THE
PROSPEROUS
PRIVATE
PRACTICE

THE
PROSPEROUS
PRIVATE
PRACTICE

A Therapist's Guide to
Launching and Growing
a Thriving Practice

NANCY COWDEN, LMFT

ILLUMIFY
MEDIA.COM

Published by
Illumify Media Global
www.IllumifyMedia.com
"Let's bring your book to life!"

Library of Congress Control Number: 2025903494

Paperback ISBN: 978-1-964251-45-5

Cover design by Debbie Lewis

Printed in the United States of America

DEDICATION

For my parents, Judith and Paul, who instilled in me the love of reading and its importance in shaping a meaningful life. Though you're no longer here, your presence and influence are felt in everything I do.

And for my sons, Alexander and Dylan, who inspired me to build a private practice that gave me the freedom and flexibility to always be there for you. You remind me every day of what truly matters and why I took this path.

This is for you, with all my love.

CONTENTS

INTRODUCTION

Congratulations! By picking up this book, you've taken the first crucial step toward launching your own private therapy practice. This decision marks the beginning of an exciting journey that will not only transform your own professional life but also profoundly impact the lives of countless individuals you'll encounter along the way.

Today, as I dropped my older son off for his first day of twelfth grade and my younger for his first day of eighth grade, I thought about the crossroads I stood at thirteen years ago:

- I wanted a career that would allow me to have the freedom and flexibility to be present for my children's milestones. (Back then, my older son was turning five and would start kindergarten later that year, and my younger son was about to turn one.)
- I also wanted to build my dream life and practice. I yearned to make a greater impact in people's lives and achieve financial success on my own terms.

The decision to start my practice wasn't an easy one. It was filled with uncertainty, self-doubt, and countless what-ifs. But as I stand here today, having run a successful practice for over twelve years, I can say that I've never regretted that decision. It has allowed me to create a life that balances my passion for therapy with my commitment to my family. It has allowed me to help countless individuals and couples navigate their own life challenges. And yes, it has provided me with the financial stability and success I had hoped for.

But my journey wasn't without challenges. There were moments of frustration when my mindset limited me because I was wishy-washy about my mission and niche and wished I had more knowledge about the business side of running a practice.

But just because I spent years figuring it out doesn't mean you need to do the same.

That's why I've written this book. I want to support and empower other therapists like you to go after your dreams, equipped with the knowledge I wish I'd had when I first started.

The Prosperous Private Practice is more than just a guide—it's a road map to creating a thriving therapy business that aligns with your values and goals. Whether you're just starting out or looking to take your existing practice to the next level, this book is designed to provide you with practical, actionable strategies for success.

In the pages that follow,

- You'll find comprehensive information on essential business skills, from navigating legal requirements to implementing effective marketing strategies.
- You'll learn how to identify and attract clients who resonate with your therapeutic methods, ensuring you can make a profound and lasting impact.
- You're read about the intricacies of financial management, helping you set appropriate fees and foster long-term growth.
- Perhaps most importantly, you'll work on cultivating a mindset of abundance and resilience, learning to view challenges as opportunities for significant professional development and personal evolution.

To get the most out of this book, I recommend reading each chapter in order and pausing at the end of each to complete the action steps before moving on. These steps are designed to help you implement what you've learned, turning insights into tangible progress. By working through the book step by step, you'll build a prosperous practice with a strong foundation and clear direction.

The goal of this book is twofold. First, I want to provide you with a solid foundation in the business aspects of running a therapy practice. Second, and perhaps more importantly, I want to instill in you the confidence and mindset necessary to succeed as an entrepreneur in the mental health field.

As you venture into this journey, remember that building a prosperous practice is not just about financial success—though that is certainly a part of it. It's about creating a business that allows you to make a meaningful impact, achieve work-life balance, and find fulfillment in your chosen profession.

Remember, the path to a prosperous practice is not always linear. There will be challenges and setbacks along the way. But with the right knowledge, mindset, and support, you can overcome these obstacles and build the practice of your dreams.

As you turn the pages of this book, I want you to feel you have a mentor and guide by your side. The strategies and insights shared here will empower you to take bold steps toward your goals, just as I did all those years ago.

So, are you ready to begin this exciting journey? Let's jump in and start building your prosperous practice!

1

IGNITING THE ENTREPRENEURIAL SPIRIT WITHIN

In 1997, I moved three thousand miles across the country, leaving behind family, friends, and the only life I'd known for twenty-three years. My dream? To get my master's degree in marriage and family counseling in sunny California and eventually open a private practice with an ocean view.

Fifteen years later, I found myself staring at the beige felt walls of my cubicle, completely unfulfilled, and wondering how I'd make it through the rest of the workday. I was working for a health care organization reviewing family treatment plans, and I felt like my job was sucking the life out of me.

A few days later, severe stomach pains landed me in the ER. It was the third consecutive Sunday I'd experienced these gut-wrenching cramps, but this time was so excruciating I had no choice but to go to the hospital.

And I couldn't have been more thrilled.

Despite the pain, one of the first things I did was call my boss's work voice mail and leave a message. "Hey, Brenda! Guess what? I'm calling you from the *hospital . . .*"

Initially, the doctor thought it was my gallbladder, but it wasn't. In fact, weeks of further testing revealed no medical cause for the persistent stomach pains.

But if I were honest with myself, I didn't need a doctor to tell me what was wrong.

Deep down, I already knew that the physical pain was my body telling me I could no longer play it safe by staying in an unfulfilling job. For too long I had pushed aside my dream of building my own practice, which would allow me to have a profound impact on clients while experiencing the freedom, flexibility, and financial success I had always envisioned.

With a newborn at home and my older son starting kindergarten soon, the need for more freedom and flexibility with my schedule became impossible to ignore. The rigid nine-to-five grind prevented me from being the truly present parent and purpose-driven professional I aspired to be.

My illness was a physical manifestation of my internal tug-of-war over pursuing my entrepreneurial dream versus playing it safe at my current unfulfilling job.

Suddenly, finding myself at a crossroads the right decision became very clear.

It was time to find the courage to leap into entrepreneurship. I was finally ready and bold enough to awaken the entrepreneurial spirit I had suppressed for so long. The idea of pursuing my dream of building a private practice energized me.

However, I soon began hearing the discouraging voice of uncertainty stirring up the kinds of fears and doubts that every aspiring entrepreneur must confront.

What if I can't find clients?

What if I don't make enough money to at least replace my current income?

How will I handle all the business aspects when I have zero experience?

These fears had kept me paralyzed and playing it safe for years.

If these concerns resonate with you, you're not alone. Deciding to take the entrepreneurial leap and start your own therapy practice can feel incredibly overwhelming, especially if running a business is as new to you as it was for me. The persistent doubts about whether you have what it takes are natural.

In that pivotal moment, though, I realized something profound: feeling underprepared or unqualified is part of the entrepreneur's journey. Those fears will never entirely disappear because you've never done this before, but they also don't have to prevent you from pursuing your vision.

The truth is that every successful entrepreneur has stood at this same crossroads, dealing with the weight of doubts and insecurities. What sets the successful ones apart is their willingness to take action in the face of uncertainty. They understand confidence and clarity come through *doing*, not *waiting* until they feel 100 percent ready.

As I reflected on my own journey, I realized that my years of clinical training and experience had already equipped me with the most important skills needed to thrive as a practice owner: building trust, providing exceptional care, and profoundly impacting lives. The rest of the business skills, marketing strategies, and operational details could all be learned along the way.

What mattered most was embracing the courage to start before I felt fully prepared. To do that, I needed to combine my purpose, expertise, and commitment to ongoing growth. If I could do *that*, I would have everything I needed to build a successful practice on my own terms.

The good news is that the same potential lies within you.

ACCEPTING THAT FEAR AND DOUBT ARE NORMAL

When I was starting my private practice, I wish I had known that I wasn't alone in experiencing fears and doubts about the journey ahead. In the years since, I've learned that these concerns are incredibly common among therapists considering the leap into private practice. I've also come to understand that these fears are a natural part of the entrepreneurial process in general. Experiencing them does not mean you are inadequate or unprepared; rather, it's a sign of your courage and readiness to step outside your comfort zone and embrace growth.

Here are some of the most common fears and doubts therapists face when considering entrepreneurship:

- Financial worries: *There are already so many therapists in private practice; what if I can't make enough income to sustain my practice and pay my bills?*
- Self-doubt about business skills: *I'm a great therapist, but can I handle the business side? It's not like I learned anything about business in graduate school!*
- Concerns about attracting clients: *How will I market myself effectively and stand out in a crowded field?*
- Worries about work-life balance: *Will running my practice consume my time and energy, leading to burnout?*
- Impostor syndrome: *Am I qualified and ready to be a practice owner? What if I fail?*

If reading any of these fears makes you wonder if I can see your thoughts, don't worry; I can't. It's just that these fears are incredibly common among therapists considering the leap into private practice. In fact, I've yet to meet a therapist who didn't deal with at least one of these concerns when starting out. We are all in this together, supporting each other in overcoming these fears.

While these fears are normal, it's essential not to let them hold you back from pursuing your dream The key is to develop strategies for confronting and managing these doubts so they don't paralyze you or keep you playing small.

REPLACING A SCARCITY MINDSET WITH AN ABUNDANCE MINDSET

One of the most powerful shifts you can make is to embrace an abundance mindset rather than a scarcity mindset. A scarcity mindset is rooted in the belief that limited resources and opportunities are available. When applied to private practice, it can fuel fears about not having enough clients or income, leading to competition and fear-based decision-making.

In contrast, an abundance mindset is grounded in the belief that there are enough opportunities and resources available for everyone. By adopting this perspective, you can approach your private practice with a sense of possibility, collaboration, and trust in your ability to attract clients and create a thriving business.

For example, a scarcity mindset might lead you to undervalue your services or hesitate to invest in your own growth and development out of fear of insufficient resources. On the other hand, an abundance mindset allows you to set your fees confidently, based on the value you provide, and invest in your growth, knowing that it will ultimately benefit your clients and your practice.

Cultivating an abundance mindset takes practice, but here are several strategies you can utilize to shift your perspective:

1. Challenge scarcity-based thoughts and reframe them in terms of abundance and possibility. For example, instead of thinking, "There aren't enough clients to go around," try, "There are an abundance of clients searching daily for a therapist with my unique skills and expertise."
2. Focus on the unique value and expertise you bring to your clients and your community. Trust that the right clients will recognize and appreciate what you have to offer.
3. Surround yourself with supportive colleagues who share a mindset of collaboration and abundance. Seek opportunities for referral relationships and joint ventures, trusting that there are enough clients for everyone.
4. Practice gratitude and acknowledge the resources and opportunities already present in your life. Celebrate your successes, no matter how small, and trust that more will come.

As you work to embrace an abundance mindset and confront your fears head-on, remember that building confidence and resilience takes time and practice. Be patient with yourself and celebrate your progress along the way.

In addition to cultivating an abundance mindset, several other key mindset shifts and entrepreneurial traits will serve you well as you build your private practice.

UNDERSTANDING YOUR NEW DUAL IDENTITY

Embracing your new dual identity as a therapist and an entrepreneur is crucial for success in private practice. Many therapists struggle with this concept, often viewing their private practice as merely a legal entity that allows them to see clients independently rather than recognizing it as a real business, like their favorite coffee shop or online store. To thrive, therapists must proudly embrace their role as entrepreneurs and develop a business mindset alongside their clinical expertise.

I wish this topic were discussed more prominently in the mental health field. When I was launching my private practice, viewing myself as an entrepreneur was never suggested to me. It wasn't until I started my second business and began investing in business coaching that I started thinking of myself as an entrepreneur. Embracing this identity has empowered me and given me a whole new level of confidence and belief in my limitless potential for business success.

Unfortunately, many therapists struggle with this dual identity because they fear that focusing on the business side of their practice will somehow diminish their role as a healer. They worry that dedicating time and energy to finances, marketing, or operational tasks will detract from their ability to provide high-quality clinical care. Some therapists even express concern that thinking about their practice in business terms feels selfish or greedy, as if prioritizing financial sustainability is at odds with their commitment to helping others.

However, these two identities, therapist and entrepreneur, can and should coexist harmoniously. In fact, embracing your role as a business owner is essential to creating a prosperous practice that allows you to help more people and make a more significant global impact. By developing a solid foundation of business skills and strategies, you can build a financially sustainable practice that supports your ongoing growth and development as a clinician.

Additionally, viewing your practice through an entrepreneurial lens enhances your ability to provide high-quality care. When you have a solid understanding of your business finances, you can make informed decisions about investing in resources that support your clients' well-being, such as training in new therapeutic approaches or upgrading your office space to create a more welcoming environment. By implementing effective marketing strategies, you can connect with the clients who are the best fit for your services and expertise, allowing you to make a more profound impact in their lives.

Embracing your identity as a therapist and an entrepreneur is not about choosing between helping others and making money. Rather, it's about recognizing that these two goals are deeply interconnected. By building a successful, sustainable business, you create the conditions that allow you to show up fully for your clients and make a meaningful difference in the world. So, let go of any fear or guilt around embracing your entrepreneurial spirit, and trust that by doing so, you are not only serving your own needs but also expanding your capacity to positively impact the lives of others.

REFRAMING THE "I'M NOT A BUSINESSPERSON" MENTALITY

One of the most common self-limiting beliefs that therapists face when starting their entrepreneurial journey is the notion that they are not "businesspeople." This mentality usually stems from the fact that we are not taught business skills in school, even though many therapists dream of running their own practice.

If you've caught yourself thinking, *I'm not a businessperson*, or *I didn't go to school for this; how am I ever going to know what to do?* know that you are in good company. Many therapists struggle with these beliefs and feel that their clinical skills and expertise don't prepare them at all for running a successful business.

It's essential for you to recognize that these are beliefs and not facts. The truth is, as a therapist, you already possess many of the skills and qualities that are essential for business success, such as

- Empathy and interpersonal skills: your ability to understand and connect with others on a deep level is invaluable when it comes to building strong relationships with clients, colleagues, and referral sources.
- Communication and listening skills: As a therapist, you are an expert in communicating complex ideas and facilitating meaningful conversations; these skills translate directly to marketing, networking, and client relations in the business world.
- Problem-solving and critical thinking: Your training has equipped you to assess challenges, develop creative solutions, and adapt to changing circumstances; these are all crucial abilities in the business world, where you'll need to solve problems and make informed decisions.
- Dedication and resilience: Your commitment to your client's well-being and your ability to persevere through challenging cases demonstrate the grit and determination needed to build a thriving practice.

While recognizing that you already possess many skills needed for business success is an essential first step, overcoming self-limiting beliefs often requires intentional effort and practice.

Here are five practical tips for challenging the "I'm not a businessperson" mentality and overcoming other common self-limiting beliefs:

1. **Educate yourself.** Seek resources, courses, and workshops designed to help therapists develop business skills and knowledge.

2. **Find a mentor or coach.** Connect with experienced therapist-entrepreneurs who have successfully navigated the challenges of building a private practice. These individuals can offer valuable guidance, support, and encouragement as you develop your business skills and confidence.

3. **Join a supportive community.** Surround yourself with like-minded therapists who are also on the entrepreneurial journey. Participate in online forums, attend networking events, and join professional groups where you can share experiences, learn from others, and build relationships with colleagues who understand the unique challenges of being a therapist-entrepreneur.

4. **Start small and celebrate your progress.** Building a successful private practice is a gradual process, and it's important to acknowledge and celebrate your progress along the way. Set achievable goals, break them down into manageable steps, and take consistent action toward building your business skills and confidence.

5. **Reframe your thinking.** When self-limiting beliefs arise, remind yourself of the unique strengths and abilities you bring to your work and focus on the opportunities for growth and learning that come with embracing your new dual identity.

Remember, becoming a successful therapist-entrepreneur is not about transforming yourself into someone you're not. It's about leveraging your existing skills and passions while developing the additional knowledge and capabilities needed to build a thriving practice. By confronting self-limiting beliefs head-on and embracing your potential as both a therapist and a business owner, you'll be well on your way to creating a prosperous practice.

As you embrace your identity as a therapist and an entrepreneur, developing a strong entrepreneurial mindset is essential for building a thriving private practice. This mindset will help you navigate entrepreneurship's unique challenges and opportunities, allowing you to approach your business with creativity, resilience, and a growth-oriented perspective.

ADOPTING AN ENTREPRENEURIAL MINDSET

An entrepreneurial mindset is characterized by several key traits and attitudes that enable success in the face of challenges and uncertainty. By cultivating this mindset, you'll be better equipped to make bold decisions, seize opportunities for growth, and build a practice that truly aligns with your values and vision.

Developing an entrepreneurial mindset involves embracing change and uncertainty, adopting a growth mindset, cultivating resilience and grit, and embracing a problem-solving approach.

In my journey as an entrepreneur, embracing these traits has been tremendously helpful in navigating the ebbs and flows of building a business.

Let's explore each of these key traits in more detail and discuss practical strategies for incorporating them into your own entrepreneurial journey.

1. Embrace change and uncertainty: At the core of developing an entrepreneurial mindset is the ability to view change and uncertainty as opportunities for growth and innovation. As an entrepreneur, you'll need to become comfortable with the idea that building a private practice often involves the unknown and making decisions without knowing all the answers.

   To cultivate this aspect of an entrepreneurial mindset,
   - Practice reframing uncertainty as an opportunity to learn, experiment, and discover new possibilities for your practice.
   - Develop a tolerance for discomfort by regularly stepping outside your comfort zone and taking calculated risks.
   - Embrace a beginner mindset, approaching new challenges with curiosity and openness rather than fear or resistance.

2. Adopt a growth mindset: Another key component of an entrepreneurial mindset is having a growth mindset, which is the belief that your abilities and skills can be developed through dedication and hard work. Adopting a growth mindset will make you more likely to view challenges as opportunities for learning and development rather than as threats to your success.

   To cultivate a growth mindset,
   - Embrace failures and setbacks as valuable learning experiences, using them to improve your approach and develop new skills.
   - Seek opportunities for ongoing education and professional development, both within the therapy field and in areas such as business, marketing, and leadership.

- Surround yourself with mentors, colleagues, and role models who embody a growth mindset and can support your learning and development.

3. Cultivate resilience and grit: Building a successful private practice requires resilience and grit, which is the ability to persevere in facing challenges and setbacks. As an entrepreneur, you'll inevitably encounter obstacles and disappointments, from slow periods in your practice to complex client cases that test your skills and emotional capacity.

   To cultivate resilience and grit,

   - Develop a support system of colleagues, mentors, and loved ones who can offer encouragement and guidance during tough times.
   - Practice self-care and prioritize activities that help you recharge and maintain balance, such as exercise, meditation, and time in nature.
   - Celebrate your successes and progress along the way, using them as a source of motivation and inspiration when faced with challenges.

4. Embrace a problem-solving mindset: As an entrepreneur, you'll be asked to solve various problems and challenges, from finding creative ways to market your practice to navigating the maze of insurance billing and reimbursement. Embracing a problem-solving mindset can help you approach these challenges with creativity, resourcefulness, and a willingness to experiment and learn.

   To cultivate a problem-solving mindset,

   - Practice breaking down complex problems into smaller, more manageable components, tackling them one step at a time.

- Seek out various perspectives and ideas from colleagues, mentors, and other professionals, using them to generate creative solutions and approaches.
- Embrace experimentation, test different strategies, and refine your approach based on feedback and results.

Developing an entrepreneurial mindset is an ongoing journey that requires intentional effort and practice. As you continue cultivating these qualities, you'll find yourself better prepared to tackle the challenges and seize the opportunities that come with building a prosperous therapy practice aligned with your values and vision.

NURTURING YOUR ENTREPRENEURIAL SPIRIT

As you navigate the challenges and triumphs of building your private practice, remember that embracing your entrepreneurial spirit is not just about creating a successful business; it's about being on a transformative journey of personal and professional growth.

When you step into your role as a therapist-entrepreneur, you open yourself up to a world of possibilities. You have the freedom to create a practice that truly aligns with your values, passions, and vision for the future. You can design your ideal work schedule, choose the clients you work with, and develop innovative services and programs that profoundly impact people's lives.

Embrace the opportunity to stretch beyond your comfort zone and develop new skills and abilities. As a private practice owner, you'll have the chance to wear many hats, from clinician to marketing strategist, and each new role will help you grow in ways you never thought possible. Embrace the learning curve and view each challenge as an opportunity to expand your knowledge and strengthen your resilience.

Most importantly, remember that by embracing your entrepreneurial spirit, you are investing in your own personal and professional growth and the well-being of your clients and community.

As you continue on this journey, trust in your ability to manage the ups and downs of entrepreneurship. Surround yourself with supportive colleagues, mentors, and loved ones who believe in your vision and cheer you on every step of the way. Celebrate your successes, learn from your setbacks, and never lose sight of the deeper purpose that drives you.

Embrace your entrepreneurial spirit with courage, curiosity, and compassion. Know that by building a practice aligned with your values and vision, you are not only creating a prosperous business but also paving the way for a fulfilling and impactful life. The journey may not always be easy, but it will be worth it for yourself, your clients, and the world you seek to change for the better.

REFLECT AND TAKE ACTION

The insights and strategies in this chapter can ignite your entrepreneurial spirit and equip you to overcome the common challenges faced by therapists transitioning into private practice.

Key Takeaways
1. Embracing your dual identity as a therapist and entrepreneur is essential for building a prosperous practice that allows you to make a greater impact in the lives of your clients and community.

2. Acknowledging and confronting common fears and doubts, such as financial worries, self-doubt about business skills, and impostor syndrome, is crucial in overcoming the barriers holding you back from pursuing your entrepreneurial dreams.

3. Cultivating an abundance mindset and reframing challenges as opportunities for growth and learning can help you approach your practice with a sense of possibility, resilience, and adaptability.

4. Recognizing that you already possess many of the skills and qualities needed for business success, such as empathy, communication, problem-solving, and dedication, can help you challenge the limiting belief that you are not a "businessperson."

5. Developing key entrepreneurial traits, such as resilience, adaptability, creativity, and a growth mindset, is an ongoing process that will serve you well as you navigate the ups and downs of building a successful practice.

Action Steps

1. Identify three limiting beliefs or fears holding you back from launching your private practice. Reframe each belief or fear from an abundance or growth mindset perspective.

2. Consider a recent success or accomplishment in your professional life, even if it seems minor, and reflect on the qualities and strengths that contributed to this positive outcome. Identify how to use these traits to face future challenges and opportunities as you build your business.

3. Choose one entrepreneurial trait you'd like to develop further, and brainstorm three concrete actions you can take to cultivate this quality in the coming weeks.
4. Seek out a supportive community of like-minded therapist-entrepreneurs, whether through online forums, local networking events, or professional associations, and commit to participating in this community to share experiences, learn from others, and build meaningful connections.

Remember, building a prosperous therapy practice is a journey of personal and professional growth. By consistently challenging limiting beliefs, embracing your dual identity, and cultivating an entrepreneurial mindset, you'll be well-equipped to navigate the path ahead with confidence, resilience, and purpose.

Celebrate the progress you've made so far, and trust in your ability to create a thriving practice that aligns with your values and vision. The world needs your unique talents and passion, and by igniting your entrepreneurial spirit, you're one step closer to impacting the lives of those you serve.

2

CRAFTING A PURPOSEFUL PRACTICE

Your decision to start a private practice as a therapist is a significant milestone in your professional journey. It's an opportunity to create a business that supports your financial goals and aligns with your deepest values and aspirations.

However, in the excitement of launching your practice, it's easy to get caught up in logistics and overlook a crucial element: crafting a solid foundation of purpose.

Your purpose is the driving force behind your practice. It's the reason—beyond earning a living—that you do what you do. Your unique blend of skills, passions, and values allows you to make a meaningful difference in the lives of your clients and your community. When you build your practice on a foundation of purpose, every aspect of your business becomes infused with meaning and direction.

Have you ever felt like you were going through the motions in your work, lacking a deeper meaning or inspiration? Have you also experienced times when you felt fully alive and engaged, knowing that you were making a real difference in the lives of others? The difference between these two experiences often comes down to one key factor: purpose.

When you operate from a place of purpose, your work becomes more than just a job or a means to an end. It becomes a calling, a way to express your unique gifts and positively impact the world. Purpose provides clarity and direction, guiding your decisions and actions toward what truly matters most.

In the context of your private practice, having a strong sense of purpose is essential for several reasons:

- **It helps you stay motivated and resilient in the face of challenges.** When you're clear on your purpose, navigating the inevitable ups and downs of running a practice becomes more manageable. You can stay focused on your bigger vision, even when faced with setbacks or distractions.
- **It enhances your sense of authenticity and presence in your work, allowing you to build deeper, more meaningful connections with your clients.** By creating a practice rooted in purpose, you cultivate trust and a stronger therapeutic bond, allowing for deeper and more meaningful results.
- **It provides a framework for making decisions that align with your values.** When you're clear on your purpose, you gain confidence in your decision-making and goal setting, ensuring your actions reflect what matters most to you.
- **It contributes to a greater sense of fulfillment and joy in your business.** Your commitment to your purpose helps you stay motivated and engaged. Plus, when you're clear on your purpose, you are more likely to attract clients who resonate with your unique approach and values, leading to more rewarding and impactful work.

When I started my private practice, I initially focused on areas where I was already considered an expert. While competent in these areas, they didn't truly inspire me. Only when I took a step back and discovered my true passion and purpose did I feel renewed confidence and excitement about my work.

Looking back, I wish I had prioritized this self-discovery process. By aligning my practice with my authentic passions and values, I could have focused solely on working with clients who truly resonated with me, experiencing greater joy and fulfillment in my work from the start. This experience taught me the importance of aligning your practice with your true purpose, as it taps into a powerful source of motivation, resilience, and fulfillment.

So, how do you go about crafting your purpose? There are four essential steps to experiencing a truly purposeful practice.

1. UNCOVERING YOUR "WHY"

The first step is to explore your "why"—the deeper reasons behind your decision to become a therapist and start a private practice.

Your "why" goes beyond the services you offer or your credentials; it's the essence of who you are and what you stand for as a therapist and a human being.

To uncover your "why," start by reflecting on your motivations for becoming a therapist and building a private practice. Consider the following questions:

- What drew you to the therapy field, and what aspects of the work bring you the most fulfillment and align with your values?

- How do you hope to make a difference in the lives of your clients and your community through your work as a therapist?
- What personal experiences or values have shaped your therapy approach and desire to help others?
- What kind of lifestyle do you envision as a private practice owner, and how do you hope to align your business with your desired financial success, abundance, freedom, flexibility, and work-life balance?
- How do you believe running your practice will contribute to your personal and professional growth and overall life satisfaction?
- What kind of impact do you hope to have on your clients, your community, and the mental health field through your work as a therapist and practice owner?

As you explore your answers to these questions, look for common threads and themes. Notice the values, beliefs, and experiences that resonate most strongly with you and feel most meaningful. These are the building blocks of your unique purpose.

For instance, one therapist I worked with who was launching her private practice, Lillian, connected her "why" to a deep-seated value around social justice and equity. She saw her role as not just helping individual clients but also working to dismantle the systemic barriers and oppressive structures that impact mental health in marginalized communities. This sense of purpose drives her to take on advocacy and outreach roles in addition to her clinical work and constantly educate herself on power, privilege, and inclusivity issues. Additionally, she views her private practice as a way to achieve financial stability and abundance, enabling her to make a more significant impact through philanthropy and community involvement.

By exploring and articulating your "why," you can create a cohesive sense of purpose that informs every aspect of your practice. Ensuring that your personal motivations, professional goals, and desired lifestyle align is essential for building a fulfilling and sustainable practice that truly reflects your unique values and aspirations.

2. DEFINING YOUR CORE VALUES

After uncovering your "why," the next step is to define your core values, which will serve as the guiding principles for your practice. Your core values shape your approach to therapy, your interactions with clients, and your business decisions.

Some common core values for therapists might include the following:

- Compassion — Treating all clients with empathy, kindness, and respect
- Integrity — Being honest, transparent, and ethical in all interactions
- Growth — Facilitating personal and professional development for yourself and your clients
- Inclusivity — Cultivating a welcoming and affirming space for diverse identities and experiences
- Collaboration — Partnering with clients to help them achieve their goals and build meaningful lives

When defining your core values, be specific and intentional. Reflect on what each value means to you and how it manifests in your work. Consider the behaviors, attitudes, and actions that align with your values and those that don't.

For example, a therapist who values inclusivity might

- pursue ongoing education and training around issues of diversity, equity, and cultural competence
- ensure that their intake forms and office space are welcoming and affirming for clients of all backgrounds and identities
- actively seek out referral relationships with providers who specialize in serving marginalized populations
- advocate for greater access and inclusivity in their community

Your core values should be the foundation for every decision you make in your practice, helping you stay true to your purpose and maintain integrity and authenticity in your work. When faced with a challenging situation or opportunity, ask yourself, *Does this align with my core values?* The answer will guide you toward choices that align with your deepest beliefs and commitments.

3. CRAFTING YOUR MISSION AND YOUR VISION

With your core values as a foundation, you can craft clear and compelling mission and vision statements for your practice. These statements serve as a road map, guiding you toward your goals and helping you stay aligned with your purpose.

A mission statement articulates the core purpose and focus of your practice. It answers the question, "What do I do, and whom do I serve?" A strong mission statement is concise and specific and captures the unique value you offer to your clients and community.

Here are a couple of examples of mission statements for therapy practices:

- "To empower women in midlife to navigate the challenges and opportunities of this transformative stage through mindfulness-based therapy, self-care strategies, and personal growth work, fostering renewed purpose, vitality, and joy."
- "To cultivate a safe, affirming practice that supports the mental health and well-being of the LGBTQ+ community through trauma-informed care, identity exploration, and personal growth while engaging in community outreach and education to foster a more inclusive society."

To craft your mission statement, consider these questions:

- What specific services or specialties do you offer?
- Who is your ideal client or target audience?
- What problems or challenges do you help your clients overcome?
- What results or outcomes do you strive to achieve through your work?

Your vision statement paints a picture of your long-term aspirations and impact. It answers the question, "What do I hope to achieve through my practice?" A compelling vision statement is inspiring and ambitious and aligns with your personal and professional values.

Here are a couple of examples of vision statements for therapy practices:

- "To create an inclusive, affirming therapy practice that celebrates diversity and provides a haven for individuals from all walks of life. By embracing a culturally sensitive approach and continuously educating myself on marginalized communities' unique experiences and challenges, I aim to help my clients heal, grow, and thrive in a world that truly values and respects their identities."
- "To cultivate a private practice that serves as a catalyst for healing, growth, and transformation in the lives of my clients. By creating a warm, welcoming space and utilizing a holistic approach that addresses the mind, body, and spirit, I aim to help individuals cultivate greater self-awareness, build healthier relationships, and lead more fulfilling, purposeful lives."

To craft your vision statement, consider these questions:

- What is the ultimate impact you want to have on your clients, your community, and the world?
- What kind of practice do you want to build over the next five, ten, or twenty years?
- How do you want to be known and remembered in your field?
- What legacy do you want to leave through your work?

Well-crafted mission and vision statements provide clarity, direction, and inspiration for your practice. They constantly remind you of your purpose and help you make decisions that align with your values and goals. By taking the time to develop these statements, you lay the foundation for a practice that is not only successful but also deeply meaningful and impactful.

4. IDENTIFYING YOUR IDEAL NICHE

Building a purposeful and prosperous practice involves identifying your ideal niche—the specific subset of the therapy market you're uniquely qualified and passionate about serving. This is where you can make the most significant impact and build a reputation as the go-to expert.

Many therapists, especially those just starting, feel pressure to be generalists and take on any client who comes their way. They fear choosing a niche will limit their potential client pool or alienate those who don't fit their specific focus. As helping professionals with big hearts, we often want to support anyone who needs our services.

When I started, choosing a niche wasn't even a topic I heard therapists discuss. I considered myself a generalist and marketed myself as a child and family therapist due to my past experience and community recognition. I was afraid to niche down further to specific problems that children or families might face because I worried it would limit my ability to attract enough clients. I didn't explore other possible niches that I might have been more passionate about because I feared I wasn't enough of an expert in them. This approach initially made me feel unfulfilled in my private practice, and I eventually realized I needed to refocus.

When I honestly evaluated my ideal clients and their issues, I was able to align my practice with my true passions and expertise. By doing so, I called in my soulmate clients and began truly to thrive in my work. This experience taught me the importance of identifying and embracing your ideal niche, even if it means stepping out of your comfort zone.

It's important to remember that niching down is not about limiting your impact or turning away people in need. In fact, it's quite the opposite. By focusing on a specific niche, you can expand your reach, attract more ideal clients, and make a greater difference in the lives of those you serve.

When you approach niching down with a scarcity mindset, it may lead to fears that you will limit your potential client base or miss out on opportunities. However, shifting to an abundance mindset allows you to recognize that plenty of clients are actively seeking the specific and unique services and approaches you offer. Choosing a niche positions you as a specialist in your field, making it easier for your ideal clients to find you and allowing you to focus on attracting those specifically looking for what you offer.

Niching down empowers you to make a greater impact in the lives of those you are passionate about serving. With a targeted focus, you can dive deeper into understanding their specific challenges, needs, and desires, tailoring your services, communication, and support to serve your niche better. This ultimately leads to more transformative experiences for your clients.

Remember, embracing an abundance mindset means recognizing that there is no shortage of opportunities or clients within your chosen niche. By specializing and delivering exceptional value to your target audience, you open the door to a thriving business that allows you to make a profound difference in the lives of those you serve.

Understanding the Difference Between a Niche and a Specialization

Having explored the importance of narrowing down and adopting an abundance mindset, let's delve deeper into understanding the difference between a niche and a specialization. As you consider the focus for your practice, it's crucial to distinguish between these two concepts, which are often used interchangeably but refer to different aspects of your professional focus.

A specialization refers to a particular area of expertise or clinical focus within the broader therapy field, often defined by a specific treatment modality, theoretical orientation, or client population. For example, a therapist might specialize in

- cognitive-behavioral therapy
- trauma-informed care
- working with children and adolescents

In contrast, a niche is a more specific subset of the therapy market that you target within your specialization. It's defined by a particular demographic, psychographic, or problem area that you're uniquely qualified and passionate about serving. For instance, within the specialization of working with children and adolescents, a therapist might choose to focus specifically on working with teenage girls struggling with anxiety and perfectionism.

While a specialization is important for establishing your professional credibility and expertise, a niche allows you to stand out in the market and attract your ideal clients. Combining your specialization with a specific niche focus will enable you to create a compelling brand that resonates deeply with the people you're meant to serve.

Consider a therapist who specializes in trauma-informed care and decides to niche down to working with

- adult survivors of childhood sexual abuse,
- first responders experiencing PTSD, and
- women who have experienced domestic violence.

By focusing on these specific populations, the therapist can develop a deep understanding of their unique challenges, needs, and experiences. They can create targeted content, resources, and services that directly address these niche markets' pain points and desires, positioning themselves as the go-to expert for individuals seeking specialized support on their healing journeys.

As you reflect on your professional journey, consider the specializations that align with your skills, training, and experience. Then, explore the potential niches within those specializations that resonate with your passions and the unique value you bring to your clients. By clarifying your specialization and niche, you'll be well on your way to building a thriving practice that makes a meaningful impact in the lives of those you serve.

Determining Your Niche

So, how do you go about determining your niche? The process involves a combination of self-reflection, market research, and strategic planning. Below are some key steps to help you identify your ideal niche.

Step 1: Reflect on your passions and interests.
- What aspects of your work as a therapist bring you the most joy and fulfillment?
- What client populations or issues do you feel most drawn to serving?
- What personal or professional experiences have shaped your unique perspective and approach?

Step 2: Consider your skills and expertise.
- What specialized training, certifications, or experience do you have that sets you apart?

- What treatment modalities or theoretical orientations do you feel most comfortable using?
- What unique strengths or talents do you bring to your work as a therapist?

Step 3: Identify underserved or high-need populations in your community.

- What client populations or issues are currently underserved in your local therapy market?
- What specific challenges or needs in your community align with your skills and interests?
- Are there any emerging trends or changes in your field that create new opportunities for specialization?

Step 4: Evaluate market demand and competition.

- Is there a demonstrated need or demand for the niche you're considering in your target market?
- Who are your main competitors in this niche, and how can you differentiate yourself from them?
- What unique value or benefits can you offer your ideal clients that address their pain points or aspirations?

Step 5: Refine and test your niche.

- Based on your reflections and research, brainstorm a few potential niche options that align with your passions, skills, and market opportunities.
- Test your niche ideas with trusted colleagues, mentors, or ideal clients to gauge their resonance and viability.
- Refine your niche based on feedback and experimentation until you land on a focus that feels authentic and feasible for your practice.

Crafting Your Niche Statement

Once you've identified your niche, it's helpful to distill it into a clear and compelling niche statement. This statement communicates the essence of your niche focus in a way that resonates with your ideal clients and referral sources.

A strong niche statement typically includes three key components:

1. Your ideal client (whom you serve)
2. The specific problem or aspiration your clients have (what they struggle with or desire)
3. The unique solution or benefit you provide (how you help them achieve their goals)

Here's a simple template for crafting your niche statement:

"I help [ideal clients] who struggle with [specific problem] to [desired outcome or benefit] through [your unique approach or solution]."

For example:

- "I help BIPOC women who face systemic barriers and discrimination to navigate workplace challenges, build resilience, and advance their careers through a culturally responsive approach that combines empowerment and advocacy."
- "I help older adults who are navigating the challenges of aging, such as retirement, health concerns, and loss, to cultivate a sense of purpose, maintain social connections, and adapt to life transitions through a holistic, age-affirming approach that promotes emotional and physical well-being."

Your niche statement is a powerful tool for communicating your value and attracting your ideal clients. Use it in your marketing materials, website copy, and elevator pitch to clearly and consistently convey your practice's specific focus and benefits.

Remember, your niche may evolve as you gain more experience and insight into your ideal clients and market. Stay open to refining and adapting your niche statement to remain aligned with your purpose and resonate with those you serve.

You can build a deeply fulfilling and financially sustainable practice by embracing the power of niching and crafting a clear, compelling niche statement. You'll attract more of your ideal clients, significantly impact your community, and create a business that aligns with your unique purpose and passions as a therapist.

Aligning Your Niche with Your Broader Purpose

Once you've identified your niche and crafted a compelling niche statement, it's important to ensure that your chosen focus aligns with your broader purpose as a therapist. Your mission and vision represent your overarching goals and aspirations for your practice and the impact you wish to make.

Take a moment to reflect on how your chosen niche fits into the bigger picture of your mission and vision. Ask yourself these questions:

How does specializing in this niche align with my core purpose as a therapist and contribute to the impact I want to have on my clients and community?

How can I leverage my niche to create meaningful change and work toward my long-term vision for my practice?

You can create a personally fulfilling and professionally impactful practice by intentionally aligning your niche with your purpose. Your niche becomes a vehicle for achieving your mission and vision, allowing you to make a more significant difference in your clients' lives.

REFLECT AND TAKE ACTION

Congratulations on completing this chapter on crafting a purposeful therapy practice! You've taken a significant step toward aligning your business with your deepest values and aspirations. Let's recap the key takeaways and explore concrete actions you can take to put these insights into practice.

Key Takeaways
1. Operating your practice from a strong sense of purpose infuses every aspect of your business with meaning and direction, guiding your decisions, fueling your motivation, and deepening your connection with clients.
2. Uncovering your "why" involves exploring your motivations, values, and aspirations as a therapist and human being and identifying the common threads forming your purpose's foundation.
3. Defining your core values helps you stay true to your purpose and maintain integrity in all aspects of your practice, from client interactions to business decisions.
4. Crafting clear mission and vision statements provides a road map for your practice, articulating your core purpose, ideal clients, and long-term impact goals.
5. Identifying your ideal niche allows you to focus your expertise, stand out in the market, and attract clients who connect deeply with your unique approach and value proposition.

Action Steps
1. Set aside time for self-reflection and journaling to explore your "why." Use the prompts in this chapter to explore your motivations, values, and aspirations as a therapist. Formulate your reflections into a concise statement that captures the essence of your purpose.
2. Brainstorm a list of your core values as a therapist and business owner. For each value, write down specific examples of how you can embody and uphold this principle in your daily practice. Post your core values in a visible place as a daily reminder of your commitments.
3. Draft your mission and vision statements using the templates and examples provided in this chapter. Share your drafts with trusted colleagues, mentors, or ideal clients for feedback and refinement. Once finalized, incorporate your mission and vision into your marketing materials and decision-making processes.
4. Reflect on your skills, interests, and market opportunities to identify potential niche focus areas for your practice. Use the niche statement template to craft a compelling message communicating your unique value to your ideal clients. Test and refine your niche through market research and experimentation.
5. Schedule regular check-ins (at least annually) to review and update your foundational elements—your "why," core values, mission, vision, and niche. Assess how your practice aligns with these elements, and make adjustments to ensure ongoing purposefulness and impact.

Building a purposeful practice is an ongoing journey of self-discovery, growth, and alignment. You'll create a practice that supports your livelihood and deeply fulfills your soul by staying connected to your "why" and consistently aligning your business with your values and vision.

Embrace the process of crafting a purposeful practice and trust that by staying true to your authentic self, you'll attract the clients, opportunities, and success that are meant for you. Your unique gifts and passions are needed in this world, and by building a practice that reflects your true purpose, you'll be able to make the meaningful impact you're here to make.

3

BUILDING A STRONG LEGAL AND BUSINESS FOUNDATION FOR YOUR PRACTICE

Congratulations on defining your purposeful practice vision! That's a significant milestone! By clarifying your purpose, you've taken a crucial step in connecting with your entrepreneurial spirit. With this important piece in place, it's time to shift our focus to the next critical aspect of starting your practice: establishing a solid legal and business foundation.

This foundation is the base upon which you'll build your practice, ensuring you have a strong, stable, and legally compliant structure to support your vision and goals. In the coming sections, we'll examine the essential components of this foundation and guide you through setting it up effectively.

While the legal and business tasks may not be the most exciting part of your entrepreneurial journey, getting these pieces right from the start is crucial for your therapy practice's long-term success and sustainability.

Your legal and business foundation serves two primary purposes:

1. Ensuring compliance: It ensures that you fully comply with all applicable laws, regulations, and ethical guidelines for your profession. This protects you, your

clients, and your practice from potential legal and financial pitfalls.

2. Facilitating smooth operations: It lays the groundwork for efficiency and growth, enabling you to focus on providing exceptional care to your clients without being burdened by administrative or legal problems.

Establishing a solid legal and business foundation involves several key steps, which we'll explore in detail throughout this chapter. Each section will build upon the last, guiding you through creating a solid business infrastructure. By the end, you'll have a compliant and professional practice that minimizes risks and maximizes your opportunities for success.

CHOOSING THE PERFECT NAME FOR YOUR PRACTICE

Transitioning from your vision to reality starts with choosing the right name for your practice. Your practice name forms the basis of your brand identity. It sets the tone for your business, reflects your values, attracts the right clients, and distinguishes you from other therapists.

Aligning Your Name with Your Purpose

In the previous chapter, we discussed defining your practice's purpose, mission, and vision. As you brainstorm potential names, keep your "why," core values, mission, vision, and ideal niche in mind.

For example, suppose your mission is to empower women in midlife to rediscover their sense of self. In that case, a name like Radiant Renewal Counseling or Midlife Metamorphosis Therapy might clearly convey that idea. Or if your practice focuses on helping couples navigate the challenges of parenthood, Connected Parenting Partners or Nurturing Family Foundations could warmly convey your specialty.

The key is to choose a name that authentically represents your practice and resonates with your ideal clients. Let your purpose guide your creativity in the naming process.

Personal Name versus Business Name

One common question therapists face when choosing a practice name is whether to use their own name (like Jane Smith Counseling) or to create a separate business name (like Harmony Mental Health Associates). The decision ultimately depends on your personal preferences and long-term goals.

Using your own name can add a personal touch and build name recognition, particularly if you already have an established reputation or network in your community. This approach fosters trust, highlights your unique expertise, and creates a personal connection with clients.

Creating a separate business name, in contrast, provides greater flexibility and scalability. It allows for easier expansion by adding other therapists or practitioners under a unified brand and can communicate your specialty or approach more effectively to potential clients.

However, using your own name ties the practice closely to your personal identity, which can limit opportunities for future expansion or sale. It may feel inconsistent when adding team members and reduce the business's appeal to potential buyers.

Similarly, while a separate business name offers scalability, it may feel less personal to clients, take more effort to establish brand recognition, and require additional administrative and legal setup. For solo practitioners with no plans to expand, this extra effort may be unnecessary.

Ultimately, your decision should align with your long-term vision for your practice and the message you want to convey to potential clients.

Professional Requirements and Restrictions: Navigating the Rules

When deciding between using your personal name or a business name, review your state's guidelines and restrictions for mental health professionals. Some states regulate the use of specific words or titles based on the practitioner's license or credentials. Check your profession's ethical guidelines and state regulations to ensure compliance, and consult with a legal professional if unsure. Addressing these considerations early helps you make an informed choice and avoid potential issues later.

Brainstorming Your Practice Name

Now it is time for the fun part—coming up with ideas! Here are several strategies to help spark your creativity:

- Word association: List words or phrases related to your practice, such as your specialty, target population, therapeutic approach, or desired outcomes—experiment with combining these words to create unique name ideas.
- Location-based names: If you have a strong connection to your local community or want to emphasize your geographic area, consider incorporating your city, neighborhood, or regional landmarks into your practice name (e.g., Downtown Counseling Collective or Mountain View Wellness Center).
- Metaphorical names: You can use metaphors or symbolism to convey the essence of your practice. For

example, a practice specializing in trauma recovery might use a name like Phoenix Rising Therapy to symbolize transformation and resilience.

- Alliteration or rhyme: Names that utilize alliteration (repeating initial sounds) or rhyme can be catchy and memorable, such as Caring Counseling Connections or Serenity Solutions.
- Acronyms: Develop an abbreviation based on the keywords or phrases that describe your practice. For example, PATH could stand for Positive Action Therapy Healing.

When brainstorming, you want to keep it simple and memorable. Choose a name that is easy to pronounce, spell, and remember so it is easy for potential clients to find you and refer you to others.

Embrace progress over perfection. While selecting the right name is important, don't let indecision hinder your progress. It's better to start with a good name and refine it over time than to delay launching your practice indefinitely in pursuit of the "perfect" name.

Choosing the Right Practice Name and Securing the Domain

After brainstorming potential names for your practice, you must ensure the name you want is legally available for use. Start by searching online and checking with your state's office that oversees business registrations to confirm the name isn't already taken by another business.

Next, you'll want to verify the name isn't trademarked. Search the U.S. Patent and Trademark Office's database of registered trademarks. Also, check any state trademark data-bases and do a general web search, as trademarks can exist without federal registration. Using a trademarked name could lead to legal troubles down the road.

Assuming the name is clear, your next step is to check if a matching dot-com domain name is available for purchase. Having a website domain that matches your practice name helps reinforce your professional brand identity and makes it easy for clients to locate.

If the ideal dot-com domain is taken by another active business using the same or similar name, you may need to consider an alternative domain extension like dot-net or dot-org. Or try a different name.

If the name you picked is already registered, trademarked, or has its dot-com domain actively used by another entity, it's best to restart your search rather than risk future conflicts. As disappointing as it can feel, putting in the effort up front prevents headaches later.

Once you've chosen an available name with no trademark issues and can secure a matching domain, register it through an accredited domain registrar service like GoDaddy, Namecheap, or Squarespace.

Understanding DBAs

Another important legal and administrative consideration related to your practice name is whether you need to file a DBA (Doing Business As).

A DBA, also known as a fictitious business name or assumed name, allows you to operate your practice under a name that differs from your legal name. You may need to file a DBA if you choose to use a separate business name instead of your personal name. The requirements for filing a DBA vary by state and local jurisdiction, but some common steps include

- checking name availability with your state and county offices
- filing the necessary DBA forms with your state and/or county
- publishing a notice of your DBA in a local newspaper, if required
- obtaining any required licenses or permits

It's essential to research the specific DBA requirements in your area and comply with all relevant regulations. Failing to file a DBA properly can lead to legal complications and may prevent you from operating your practice under your chosen name.

Finalizing Your Practice Name

Choosing a practice name that aligns with your purpose, resonates with your ideal clients, and meets legal requirements is a significant milestone in establishing your business foundation.

With your practice name finalized, you've laid the groundwork for your brand identity and are ready to make the next crucial decision: choosing the right practice model for your business.

In the following section, we'll explore the pros and cons of different practice models, such as in-office, virtual, or hybrid. Understanding these options will help you determine the best fit for your services, target clients, and personal preferences.

By selecting a practice model that aligns with your goals and values, you'll create a strong foundation for your business and be well-positioned to establish your legal structure, obtain necessary licenses and permits, and confidently launch your practice.

So, let's dive in and discover the perfect practice model for your unique vision and circumstances!

CHOOSING THE RIGHT PRACTICE MODEL FOR YOUR BUSINESS

It's time to tackle another big decision: choosing the best practice model for your unique needs and goals.

When it comes to practice models, you've got three main options to choose from:

1. In-Office Practice. This is where you'll see clients face-to-face at a physical location.
2. Virtual Practice. With this model, your practice operates entirely online, and you'll conduct therapy sessions via a secure telehealth platform.
3. Hybrid Practice. This model offers the best of both worlds, as you can offer in-person and virtual sessions based on your client's preferences and needs.

Consider these key factors when choosing your practice model:

1. Target population: Select a model that resonates with your ideal client's preferences.
2. Therapy modalities: Ensure your therapeutic approaches align with the chosen model's format.
3. Personal preferences: Opt for a model that supports your work-life balance, flexibility, and comfort level.
4. Financial factors: Choose a model that fits your budget, considering start-up and ongoing costs.
5. Growth potential: Assess how each model aligns with your long-term expansion plans.

6. Regulations and licensing: Ensure compliance with relevant state regulations and licensing requirements, especially for virtual services.

These factors will help you determine the optimal practice model for your unique circumstances.

ESTABLISHING YOUR BUSINESS ADDRESS

Once you've decided on your practice model, the next step is to establish your official business address. This address will be used for legal documentation, registrations, and public information about your practice. The type of address you need depends on your chosen model.

In-Office Practice. If you offer in-person sessions, your business address will be the physical location where you meet with clients.

Virtual Practice. Even though you don't see clients in person, you will still need an official business address for registration purposes. A virtual address service is often the best solution, as it provides a physical street address (not a PO Box) that meets most state requirements for business registration. This address can be used for managing official correspondence and maintaining a professional image. Before securing a business address, verify your state's specific requirements to ensure compliance.

Hybrid Practice. Use your physical office as the primary business address for combined in-office and virtual services.

With your practice name, model, and business address in place, you've laid the groundwork for your legal and professional identity. Next, we'll explore choosing the proper business entity structure, which impacts your liability, taxes, and administrative responsibilities.

CHOOSING THE RIGHT BUSINESS
ENTITY STRUCTURE

As a mental health professional starting a private practice, selecting the appropriate business structure is a critical decision that will impact your legal responsibilities, tax obligations, and overall practice management. The following are the most common business structures for mental health practitioners.

Sole Proprietorship

A sole proprietorship is the simplest business structure, where you own and operate your practice alone. Setting up is easy and inexpensive, and you have complete control over business decisions. You report your business income and expenses on your personal tax return. However, you are personally responsible for any business debts or legal issues. This structure is best for mental health providers who are just starting, want complete control, and plan to keep their practice small. To set up a sole proprietorship, obtain the necessary business licenses and permits from your local city or county government.

Partnership

A partnership is a business owned by two or more mental health providers who share profits, losses, and management duties. It's easy and inexpensive to set up, and the business income is reported on your personal tax returns. However, all partners are personally liable for business debts and legal issues. This structure works well for mental health providers who want to collaborate and share resources. To start a partnership, create an agreement outlining roles, responsibilities, and profit-sharing, and obtain the necessary business licenses and permits.

Limited Liability Company (LLC) and Professional Limited Liability Company (PLLC)

A Limited Liability Company (LLC) is a business structure that protects your personal assets, such as your home and savings, from being used to pay business debts or legal claims. It offers flexibility in how your business income is taxed, giving you the option to be taxed as a sole proprietorship, partnership, or corporation.

A Professional Limited Liability Corporation (PLLC) is a type of LLC specifically designed for licensed professionals, such as mental health providers. Some states require professionals to form a PLLC instead of a standard LLC, while other states don't allow PLLCs at all. In states like California, mental health professionals cannot form LLCs or PLLCs and must choose a different structure, such as a sole proprietorship, partnership, or Professional Corporation (PC).

Both LLCs and PLLCs are more expensive to set up and maintain than a sole proprietorship, but they provide liability protection and flexible tax options, making them a good choice for mental health providers who want to protect their personal assets while enjoying tax benefits.

To set up an LLC or PLLC, check your state's requirements, file articles of organization with your state, and create an operating agreement outlining how your business will be run.

Professional Corporation (PC)

A Professional Corporation (PC) is designed for licensed professionals, such as mental health providers. It offers liability protection for personal assets and tax benefits. However, PCs can be more complex and costly to set up and maintain compared to other structures. One potential draw-back is the risk of double taxation, where your corporation pays taxes on its income and you also pay taxes on your salary and dividends.

This structure is ideal for professionals who want liability protection, potential tax advantages, and the added credibility of a professional corporate image. To form a PC, you must file articles of incorporation with your state, draft corporate bylaws, and hold required organizational meetings. It is important to note that specific requirements and regulations for forming a PC can vary by state and profession.

C Corporation

A C Corporation provides strong liability protection but is more complex and costly to set up and maintain. It's subject to double taxation and is best suited for large practices planning to raise significant capital or offer employee stock options. Most mental health providers will not need this structure unless they plan to grow their practice significantly. To set up a C Corporation, file articles of incorporation with your state, create corporate bylaws, hold organizational meet-ings, and issue stock.

S Corporation

An S Corporation is a business structure that offers liability protection for your personal assets and provides significant tax advantages. Unlike a traditional corporation (C Corporation), an S Corporation avoids double taxation. This means the business itself doesn't pay corporate taxes; instead, profits, losses, deductions, and credits are passed directly to your personal tax return, where they are taxed at your individual rate.

For practice owners, this structure can reduce self-employment taxes by allowing you to pay yourself a salary (subject to payroll taxes) and take additional profits as distributions, which are not subject to the same taxes. However, S Corporations have strict eligibility requirements, such as limits on the number of shareholders, and come with more administrative responsibilities as compared to a sole proprietorship or LLC.

To set up an S Corporation, you must first form a corporation or LLC, then file Form 2553 with the IRS to elect S Corporation status. This structure is particularly beneficial for mental health providers seeking both liability protection and tax savings.

Checking State-Specific Requirements

Before finalizing your business structure choice, verifying state-specific regulations for mental health private practices is essential. Start by checking your state's Secretary of State website to determine which business entities are permitted for licensed mental health professionals. Some states restrict certain entity types, such as LLCs, for licensed professionals. The Secretary of State's website will also guide you through filing the necessary formation documents, such as Articles of Organization or Incorporation, and explain any associated fees. This step ensures that your chosen structure is allowed in your state and that you file all required paperwork accurately.

Consulting with Legal and Financial Professionals

Consult legal and financial experts who understand your state's laws. They can help you choose the best business structure. The right structure will limit liability, minimize taxes, and allow for growth while avoiding unnecessary complexity.

Once you decide on the business structure, you must obtain the required legal IDs and permits to operate your practice.

OBTAINING IMPORTANT BUSINESS REGISTRATIONS AND LICENSES

With your business structure selected, the next crucial steps involve obtaining key registrations and licenses required for legally operating your private practice. Let's go through the important ones.

Getting Your Employer Identification Number (EIN)

An Employer Identification Number (EIN) is a unique "tax ID" assigned to your business by the Internal Revenue Service (IRS). You need an EIN for various important purposes:

- To form a corporation, partnership, or LLC with multiple members
- To hire and report wages and withholdings for any employees
- To open a separate business bank account and keep finances separate
- To use instead of your social security number for added privacy

Obtaining an EIN is straightforward and free. You can apply online directly at the IRS website to receive your EIN immediately, or file Form SS-4 by mail or fax, which takes around four weeks to process.

Be sure to keep your EIN secure, as you'll need to provide it for tax filings, business bank accounts, and many other purposes. If you have any questions, consult a tax professional for guidance on using your EIN properly.

Securing Local Business Licenses and Permits for Your Practice

After obtaining your EIN, the next crucial step is securing the required business licenses and permits from your local government to operate your practice legally.

Operating with the necessary licenses and permits is essential because it

- ensures you follow all legal regulations for your profession
- verifies you meet health, safety, and zoning requirements
- demonstrates your practice's legitimacy and professionalism to clients

To get properly licensed and permitted, you must take several steps:

1. Contact your city/county clerk's office to determine the exact requirements.
2. Gather documents like your professional license, business registration, and office lease or deed.
3. Submit completed applications, documentation, and fees to the appropriate offices.
4. Once approved, prominently display licenses/permits in your office as required.

Failing to obtain proper licensing can result in fines, legal issues, or being barred from operating. If any questions arise, consult legal or professional resources.

With business licenses and permits secured, you'll be well positioned to run a compliant professional practice. The next step is obtaining your National Provider Identifier (NPI).

Getting Your National Provider Identifier (NPI)

The next important step is obtaining your National Provider Identifier (NPI), a unique ten-digit "health care ID number" assigned by the Centers for Medicare and Medicaid Services (CMS).

As a mental health practitioner, you need an NPI for

- billing insurance and getting reimbursed
- credentialing with insurance panels and health systems
- maintaining HIPAA compliance
- establishing your professional identity

There are two types:

1. NPI Type 1 (Individual) – Issued specifically for individual health care providers. This NPI number follows you as a provider throughout your career, regardless of location, practice, or business structure changes. It identifies you personally as a health care professional for billing and claims purposes.
2. NPI Type 2 (Organizational) – Issued for business entities that provide health care services, such as group practices, clinics, or mental health practices that have incorporated as an LLC, PC, or other entity. This NPI is associated with the business itself rather than an individual provider.

To apply for your Individual NPI, use the fast online application via the NPPES website (get NPI immediately) or file paper Form CMS-10114 by mail (takes around four to six weeks).

Provide accurate details like name, business address, specialty taxonomy code, and license information.

With your NPI obtained along with other registrations, you'll have the core provider identifiers needed to operate compliantly and start seeing clients in your private practice.

However, before opening your doors to clients, you must protect yourself and your practice with the right insurance coverage. In the next section, we'll discuss the importance of securing malpractice and liability insurance to safeguard your professional assets and reputation.

SECURING MALPRACTICE AND PROFESSIONAL LIABILITY INSURANCE

Before opening your private practice, you must obtain malpractice and professional liability insurance (also called errors and omissions or E&O insurance). This critical coverage protects your practice from legal claims related to negligence or failure to provide appropriate care. Specifically, it serves several functions:

- Protects your finances against legal fees, settlements, judgments
- Meets requirements set by insurance panels, health systems, landlords
- Demonstrates your professionalism and responsibility
- Provides peace of mind so you can focus on caring for clients

To help you identify the best insurance provider and plan for your practice, take these steps:

1. Research providers specializing in mental health professional liability policies
2. Compare coverage limits, deductibles, premiums
3. Evaluate your practice's unique risks to secure adequate coverage
4. Complete the application process, providing key practice details
5. Maintain active coverage through timely premium payments

With malpractice and liability insurance secured and other legal and business foundations in place, you can confidently launch a well-protected private practice.

SEPARATING BUSINESS AND PERSONAL FINANCES

With insurance secured, the next crucial step is setting up a dedicated business bank account to separate your practice finances from personal accounts. Doing this provides you with the following benefits:

- Ensures tax compliance and simplifies expense tracking
- Protects personal assets from legal claims or creditors
- Enables financial monitoring for growth decisions
- Allows easy identification of business tax deductions

Unlike opening a personal account with a couple of forms of ID, opening a business account means providing documents related to your business. Luckily, the process is straightforward:

1. Gather documents like your EIN, business registration, licenses

2. Compare banks for amenities like low fees, online banking, bookkeeping tools
3. Provide the required information and fund the initial deposit
4. Set up online banking and accounting software integration

Separating accounts lays the foundation for organized financial management and asset protection. It's a crucial step in establishing your professional private practice.

Chapter 5 will cover broader financial planning aspects like budgeting, bookkeeping, and taxes. For now, celebrate checking off this key milestone!

REFLECT AND TAKE ACTION

Congratulations on completing this chapter on setting up a solid legal and business foundation for your private practice! By taking the time to understand and implement these critical steps, you're setting up your practice for long-term success, professionalism, and compliance.

Before we wrap up, let's recap the key takeaways and explore some concrete actions you can take to put these insights into practice.

Key Takeaways
- Choosing a memorable, meaningful, and legally available practice name is crucial to your brand identity and sets the tone for your business.
- Selecting the right practice model (in-office, virtual, or hybrid) and establishing a compliant business address are important decisions that impact your operations, client population, and professional image.

- Understanding the advantages, disadvantages, and legal requirements of different business structures (sole proprietorship, partnership, LLC, PLLC, PC, C Corp, S Corp) allows you to choose the best option for your unique needs and goals.
- Filing the necessary paperwork with your state, obtaining an Employer Identification Number (EIN), and securing a National Provider Identifier (NPI) are essential steps in legally establishing your business entity and complying with tax and health care requirements.
- Securing local business licenses, permits, and professional liability insurance protects your practice and demonstrates your commitment to legal compliance and ethical standards.
- Setting up a separate business bank account helps maintain clear boundaries between your personal and professional finances and simplifies record-keeping.

Action Steps

1. Brainstorm potential practice names that align with your brand identity, target population, and unique value proposition. Research their availability and secure your domain.
2. Evaluate your target population, service offerings, and personal preferences to determine your business's best practice model. Establish a compliant business address that meets your state's requirements and protects your privacy.
3. Consult with legal and financial professionals to assess the pros and cons of different business structures for your specific situation. Choose the structure that

provides the best balance of liability protection, tax benefits, and simplicity for your practice.

4. File the necessary paperwork with your state to legally form your chosen business entity. Apply for an EIN through the IRS website or by submitting Form SS-4. Obtain an NPI by applying through the NPPES website or submitting Form CMS-10114.

5. Contact your local city or county offices to identify and obtain your practice's required business licenses and permits. Research and secure a professional liability insurance policy that adequately protects your business and meets contractual requirements.

6. Open a separate business bank account and credit card to maintain clear boundaries between your personal and professional finances. Implement a system for tracking income, expenses, and other key financial metrics.

Taking these steps lays a solid legal and business foundation. This supports your practice's long-term success, credibility, and growth potential. Investing time and effort into this foundation is essential for building a sustainable practice.

Establishing this foundation is an ongoing process. As your practice grows, stay proactive in addressing new challenges and opportunities. Staying informed, adaptable, and true to your vision will help you navigate building a successful practice that makes a positive impact.

With the legal and business foundation in place, we will next focus on your financial empowerment. This includes identifying and challenging limiting beliefs, developing an abundance mindset, and embracing financial success as a natural and necessary part of building a thriving practice.

4

CULTIVATING A PROSPEROUS MONEY MINDSET

Your ability to challenge beliefs that are negatively impacting your financial success as a mental health professional is foundational to empowering you to create a prosperous practice.

We enter this field because we have a passion for helping others, but we can buy into the misconception that this means we shouldn't desire wealth and abundance. After all, a common message in our society is that people in helping professions shouldn't think about making money—and that those who do must be greedy and wrong.

To make matters worse, graduate programs often focus heavily on clinical skills and theory, with little to no attention paid to the business and financial aspects of running a private practice. Ill-equipped to navigate the financial realities of private practice, therapists are even more vulnerable to limiting beliefs about money, undervaluing their services, and experiencing financial stress.

It's essential for therapists to pursue financial education resources, such as books, workshops, courses, and mentors, to build a strong foundation for financial success in private practice. By prioritizing financial education and developing a solid understanding of business and money management principles, therapists can break free from limiting financial beliefs and create a more sustainable and fulfilling practice.

Let's look at some techniques to identify and rewrite these limiting beliefs and help you develop a new money mindset that embraces abundance.

IDENTIFYING LIMITING BELIEFS ABOUT FINANCES

Have you been told, implicitly or explicitly, that it's greedy or unethical to desire financial success? Or that focusing on money takes away from your ability to provide genuine care? Or that that wealth is not in line with a life of service?

If you have received and internalized limiting messages about the role of money in the helping professions, they may be showing up in your practice in the following ways:

- You set your fees too low and feel guilty when you want to raise them.
- You feel uncomfortable discussing money with your clients.
- You believe that struggling financially is part of being in this field.
- You think you don't deserve financial success.
- You actively avoid dealing with the business side of your private practice, especially managing anything related to your finances and long-term financial health.

You're not alone if you have adopted any of these beliefs or practices. Many therapists have concerns about embracing financial abundance, such as the fear of being perceived as greedy or the belief that money corrupts.

I can tell you from personal experience that these limiting beliefs are very real, and I have had to face and overcome each one of them.

When I was in graduate school, I vividly remember being told by a mentor not to expect to make money as a therapist. They went on to say not to expect to get rich by going into private practice and, in fact, to expect to have to take on additional jobs to make ends meet. I was shocked when she shared this with us. It had never occurred to me that I would have to struggle financially as a therapist.

My mistake at the time was not questioning this information and believing what this person said to be fact because they had been in the field for years.

As a result of messages like this and others that followed, my beliefs about money and my value and worth as a therapist were formed. Consequently, when I got my first job out of graduate school, I didn't think twice about being paid eleven dollars an hour. I was even excited when I got my next job making a mere $26,000 a year. I rationalized these low wages by telling myself, *I'm just an intern, so I have to pay my dues and get my hours for licensure. I have no place to complain.* Or *I shouldn't be thinking about making money when so many people who need my help are struggling.*

One of the reasons I waited so long to start a private practice was that I was still haunted by my mentor's words, who had told us that we could never survive on the income from a private practice alone. A scarcity mindset had its hold on me for a long time.

Although I eventually started my practice despite these messages, I soon realized that if I was going to thrive financially, I needed to face these deep-seated limiting beliefs I had about money, wealth, and my worth as a therapist.

Let's address these common objections head-on:

1. *Desiring financial success makes me greedy.*
   - Reframe: Desiring financial success allows you to create a sustainable practice that enables you to serve your clients more effectively and positively impact your community.
2. *Focusing on money takes away from my ability to provide genuine care."*
   - Reframe: When you have a financially stable practice, you can focus more fully on providing high-quality care to your clients without the added stress and distraction of financial struggles.
3. *Money corrupts and is not in line with a life of service.*
   - Reframe: Money is a tool that can be used for good. By building a financially successful practice, you can invest in your professional development, offer pro bono services, and contribute to causes that align with your values of service and positive change.

By addressing these objections and reframing them in a way that aligns with your values as a therapist, you can shift your mindset and embrace the idea that financial abundance is acceptable and necessary for creating a thriving and impactful practice.

UNDERSTANDING THE CONNECTION BETWEEN FINANCIAL EMPOWERMENT AND SELF-CARE

Financial stress and limiting beliefs about money can take a significant toll on therapists' well-being, contributing to burnout, anxiety, and poor self-care. When we are constantly worried about making ends meet or feeling guilty about desiring financial success, it becomes challenging to prioritize our own needs and maintain a healthy work-life balance.

On the other hand, cultivating a prosperous money mindset and building a financially thriving practice can enable therapists to prioritize their self-care and well-being. When we have a stable and abundant income, we can invest in activities and resources that support our physical, emotional, and mental health, such as

- engaging in regular self-care practices like exercise, meditation, or hobbies
- attending workshops and retreats for personal and professional growth
- seeking our own therapy or coaching to process challenges and maintain well-being
- taking time off for rest, relaxation, and rejuvenation without financial guilt

By prioritizing our own self-care and well-being, we become better equipped to show up fully and provide high-quality care to our clients. Financial empowerment and self-care are interconnected, and by nurturing both, we can create a sustainable and fulfilling practice that allows us to thrive both personally and professionally.

DEVELOPING A NEW MONEY MINDSET

In order for us to feel financially empowered as mental health professionals, we must confront and challenge our long-held assumptions and beliefs about money and develop a new money mindset. We need a mindset rooted in abundance and the belief that desiring or having money does not make us greedy and isn't something we should feel guilty or ashamed about having.

To develop a new, healthier relationship with money, we must first acknowledge our worth as mental health professionals and believe that achieving financial abundance is not at odds with the desire to help others and make a meaningful impact in our communities. We can care deeply for our clients and their well-being and also build a financially thriving practice.

When we overcome our money blocks and develop a mindset of abundance, we open ourselves up to experiencing tremendous growth and extensive impact. We put ourselves in a financial position to invest in our own professional development, create more accessible and affordable services, and contribute to causes that align with our values.

1. Overcome Impostor Syndrome and Own Your Worth

One common challenge that many therapists face when it comes to embracing financial abundance is impostor syndrome. Impostor syndrome is the feeling of self-doubt and the belief that one's successes are due to luck or fraud rather than skill and expertise. This can lead therapists to undervalue their services, struggle with fee setting, and feel undeserving of financial success.

To overcome impostor syndrome and own your worth as a therapist, consider the following strategies:

- Acknowledge your expertise and the value you provide to your clients. Remind yourself of your education and training and the positive impact you have on their lives.
- Focus on the transformations and outcomes you help your clients achieve rather than comparing yourself to others or dwelling on self-doubt.

- Surround yourself with supportive colleagues who affirm your worth and value as a therapist. Seek mentors or join a community of like-minded professionals who can provide encouragement and guidance.
- Practice self-compassion and reframe negative self-talk. When impostor syndrome thoughts arise, counter them with evidence of your skills, knowledge, and the difference you make in your clients' lives.

By actively working to overcome impostor syndrome and owning your worth, you can develop the confidence and self-assurance needed to embrace financial abundance and build a thriving practice.

2. Rewrite Your Money Beliefs

To begin cultivating financial empowerment, it's essential to identify and challenge the limiting money beliefs that may hold you back and actively reinforce your values and self-worth. Here are some powerful techniques to help you develop and maintain a new, empowering money mindset:

- **Journal about your money mindset.** Set aside time to write about your thoughts, feelings, and money-related experiences. Note any recurring themes, fears, or limiting beliefs that come up for you. By bringing your subconscious beliefs to the surface, you can begin examining and challenging them.

  Not sure what to write about? Reflect on your earliest memories and experiences related to money. What messages did you receive from your family, culture, or society about wealth and financial success? How have these early experiences shaped your current beliefs and behaviors around money? By understanding the roots of your money beliefs, you can start to untangle them and create new, empowering narratives.

After you have identified your limiting money beliefs, take the time to reframe them in a more empowering way. For example, if you find yourself thinking, *It's selfish to want financial success as a therapist*, reframe it as *Financial success allows me to have a greater positive impact on my clients and community*. You can shift your mindset and actions toward financial empowerment by consciously rewriting your beliefs.

- **Look for financial role models.** Seek out therapists and other helping professionals who have achieved financial success while maintaining their values and integrity. Connect with them and study their mindsets, strategies, and approaches to money. When you surround yourself with positive financial role models, it will become easier to internalize the belief that it's possible to create a thriving practice while making a difference in the world.

- **Create a money mantra.** This is a fun one. Create a personal money mantra that will help you reinforce your new, empowering beliefs about your worthiness for financial success. Your mantra should be a short and personally powerful phrase that you can repeat daily and turn to during times of doubt or when faced with uncomfortable financial decisions. Examples might include, "I am worthy of wealth and abundance," or "Prosperity supports my purpose."

- **Celebrate your financial wins.** Be sure to acknowledge and celebrate your financial successes, no matter how small. Whether it's attracting a new client, reaching a monthly revenue goal, or putting money aside for a dream trip, take a moment to acknowledge and appreciate your achievements. By consistently celebrating your financial wins, you'll build momentum and confidence in your ability to create a prosperous practice.

3. *Shift Your Mindset about Navigating Financial Challenges*

Building a financially thriving practice is not without its challenges. Therapists may face inconsistent income, unexpected expenses, or economic downturns that can create financial stress and uncertainty. However, cultivating a prosperous money mindset can help you navigate these challenges with resilience, creativity, and a focus on growth opportunities.

Here are some mindset shifts that can help you approach financial challenges in a more empowered way:

- **Embrace a growth mindset.** View financial challenges as opportunities for learning and growth rather than setbacks or failures. Ask yourself, *What can I learn from this experience? How can I use this challenge to become a better therapist and business owner?*
- **Focus on what you can control.** When faced with financial challenges, it's easy to feel overwhelmed and powerless. Instead, focus on the aspects of your practice and finances you can control, such as your marketing efforts, fee structure, and expenses. You can create a sense of empowerment and forward momentum by taking proactive steps in these areas.
- **Cultivate a solutions-oriented approach**. Rather than dwelling on the problem or engaging in negative self-talk, focus on finding creative solutions. Brainstorm ideas, seek advice from mentors or colleagues, and be

open to new approaches. Remember, every challenge is an opportunity to innovate and grow.

- **Practice gratitude and abundance.** Even in the face of financial challenges, consciously focus on the abundance and opportunities in your life. Be thankful for your skills, clients, and the positive impact you make in the world. By maintaining an abundance mindset, you'll be better equipped to weather any financial storms and emerge stronger and more resilient.

As you cultivate a prosperous money mindset and build a financially thriving practice, it is important to ensure that your financial goals align with your personal and professional values. When your financial pursuits are in harmony with your deeper purpose and values, you'll experience greater fulfillment, motivation, and success.

Take some time to reflect on your values and how they can inform your financial goals and decision-making in your practice. Consider questions such as

- *What is most important to me in my work as a therapist?*
- *How can I use my financial success to impact my clients and community positively?*
- *What causes or issues am I passionate about, and how can I align my financial goals with supporting these causes?*

Once you have clarity on your values, look for ways to integrate them into your financial goals and practices. Here are some examples:

- Set aside a portion of your income for pro bono work or sliding scale fees to ensure accessibility for under-served populations.
- Invest in socially responsible funds or donate a percentage of your profits to organizations that align with your values.
- Use your financial success to create opportunities for personal and professional growth, such as attending workshops or retreats that deepen your skills and increase your impact as a therapist.

By aligning your financial goals with your values, you'll create a sense of purpose and meaning in your financial pursuits, and you'll be more likely to experience fulfillment and success in your practice.

CULTIVATING A SUPPORTIVE COMMUNITY FOR FINANCIAL EMPOWERMENT

Cultivating a prosperous money mindset and building a financially thriving practice can be a challenging journey. It's essential to surround yourself with a supportive community of colleagues who share your values and aspirations. When you have a network of like-minded professionals to turn to for encouragement, advice, and accountability, you'll be better equipped to overcome obstacles and stay committed to your financial goals.

Below are some ways to cultivate a supportive community for financial empowerment.

Join or create a mastermind group.

Seek out or start a small group of therapists committed to building financially successful practices while maintaining their values and integrity. Meet regularly to share challenges, celebrate successes, and provide mutual support and accountability.

Participate in online communities.

Engage in online forums, social media groups, or professional networks where therapists discuss the business and financial aspects of private practice. Share your experiences, ask questions, and learn from the wisdom and insights of others.

Attend workshops and conferences.

Seek out workshops, conferences, or retreats that focus on the financial and business aspects of private practice. These events provide opportunities to learn from experts, connect with like-minded colleagues, and expand your support network.

Find an accountability partner.

Partner with a colleague who shares your financial goals and values, and commit to checking in regularly with each other to share progress, challenges, and encouragement. Having a dedicated accountability partner can help you stay focused and motivated on your journey toward financial empowerment.

―⁓―

By cultivating a supportive community, you'll gain access to valuable resources, insights, and encouragement to help you navigate the challenges and opportunities of building a financially thriving practice. Remember, you don't have to do this alone—there is a community of like-minded therapists who are eager to support and inspire you on your journey.

Remember, cultivating financial empowerment and a new money mindset is an ongoing journey, not a one-time event. By consistently applying these techniques and strategies, you'll gradually transform your relationship with money and build a strong foundation for a financially successful and impactful practice.

REFLECT AND TAKE ACTION

Congratulations on completing this chapter on cultivating a prosperous money mindset! By exploring and challenging your beliefs about money, you've taken an important step toward creating a financially thriving and fulfilling practice. Developing a healthy relationship with money is essential for sustaining your work as a therapist and increasing your impact on the lives of others.

Before we move forward, let's review the key takeaways and explore actionable steps to put these insights into practice.

Key Takeaways
- Identifying and challenging limiting money beliefs is crucial for developing an abundance mindset that allows you to embrace your worth as a therapist and build a financially thriving practice.
- Developing a new money mindset involves acknowledging your value as a mental health professional and believing that financial success is not at odds with your desire to help others and make a meaningful impact.
- Techniques such as money mindset journaling, finding financial role models, creating a money mantra, and celebrating your financial wins can help you cultivate and maintain an empowering money mindset.

- Overcoming impostor syndrome and owning your worth as a therapist are essential for embracing financial abundance and building a thriving practice.
- Cultivating a supportive community of like-minded professionals can provide valuable resources, insights, and encouragement on your journey toward financial empowerment.

Action Steps
1. Set aside time for money mindset journaling. Write down your thoughts, feelings, and experiences related to money, and identify any limiting beliefs holding you back.
2. Seek out and connect with therapists and other helping professionals who have achieved financial success while maintaining their values and integrity. Learn from their mindsets, strategies, and approaches to money.
3. Create a personal money mantra that reinforces your new, empowering beliefs about your worthiness for financial success. Repeat this mantra daily and turn to it during times of doubt or when faced with uncomfortable financial decisions.
4. Start acknowledging and celebrating your financial successes, no matter how small. By consistently recognizing your achievements, you will build momentum and confidence in creating a prosperous practice.
5. Join or create a supportive community of therapists who share your values and aspirations for building financially thriving practices. Engage in mastermind groups, online communities, workshops, or accountability partnerships to gain encouragement, advice, and inspiration.

Now that you have cultivated a prosperous money mindset and developed a strong foundation for financial success, it's time to dive into the practical aspects of building a financially empowered practice. In the following chapter, we will explore the key decisions and strategies to help you create a sustainable and thriving business, including choosing the right payment model, setting aligned fees, budgeting for start-up and ongoing expenses, navigating insurance credentialing, and creating a financial road map for long-term success.

As you begin this journey, remember that building a financially empowered practice is an ongoing process that requires commitment, flexibility, and a willingness to learn and adapt. By applying the principles and strategies outlined in the next chapter, you'll be well-equipped to make informed decisions that support your financial well-being and allow you to make a lasting impact in your clients' lives.

5

BUILDING A FINANCIALLY EMPOWERED PRACTICE

Now that you have cultivated a prosperous money mindset, it's time to discuss the practical aspects of building a financially empowered practice.

In this chapter, we will explore the key decisions and strategies that will help you create a sustainable and thriving business. These include choosing the right payment model, setting aligned fees, budgeting for start-up and ongoing expenses, navigating insurance credentialing, and creating a financial road map for long-term success.

As you begin this journey, remember that building a financially empowered practice is an ongoing process that requires commitment, flexibility, and a willingness to learn and adapt. By applying the principles and strategies outlined in this chapter, you'll be well-equipped to make informed decisions that support your financial well-being and allow you to make a lasting impact in your clients' lives.

EVALUATING AND CHOOSING A PAYMENT MODEL

Choosing a payment model is one of the most important decisions you'll make when setting up your private practice. The three main payment models for mental health professionals are insurance-based, private pay, and hybrid. Each model has advantages and disadvantages, and the right choice for your practice will depend on factors such as the population you want to work with, financial goals, and personal preferences.

Insurance-Based Model

In an insurance-based model, you contract with one or more insurance companies and accept reimbursement for services provided to covered clients. Advantages of this model include

1. A broader client base: Accepting insurance can make your services more accessible to a larger pool of potential clients who might not otherwise be able to afford therapy.
2. A steady referral stream: Insurance companies often provide referrals, which can help you build and maintain a consistent caseload.

However, there are significant disadvantages to consider:

1. Lower reimbursement rates: Insurance companies typically reimburse at lower rates than private-pay fees, which can impact your overall revenue.
2. Administrative burden: Dealing with insurance paperwork, checking client benefits, and filing claims can be time-consuming and confusing.
3. Constraints on treatment: Insurance companies often limit the type, frequency, and duration of treatment they will cover based on a client's benefits plan. They can also dictate which diagnoses they will cover for reimbursement, limiting what you can treat.

4. Unreliable payment frequency: Insurance reimbursements can be unpredictable and subject to delays, denials, and other administrative hurdles. This can result in inconsistent cash flow and increased financial stress for therapists.
5. Potential for audits: Insurance companies may conduct audits of your client records and billing, which can be stressful and time-consuming and may result in them taking back money they had previously paid you.

Private Pay Model

In a private-pay model, clients pay you directly for services on the day they are provided. Advantages of this model include

1. Setting your own fees: You have the freedom to set your fees, which will be higher than insurance reimbursement rates. This gives you the option to see fewer clients while maintaining the same income you would earn with insurance or to see the same number of clients and earn significantly more.
2. No constraints on treatment: Without insurance restrictions, you have more flexibility in determining the course and duration of treatment based on your clients' needs.
3. Easy billing: Collecting payment from private pay clients can be a simple and quick process.

Disadvantages of the private-pay model include

1. Narrower client base: Adopting a private-pay model may limit your potential client pool to those who can

afford to pay out-of-pocket, depending on your fees and location.

2. Increased marketing efforts: Without the referral stream provided by insurance companies, you may need to invest more time and resources into marketing your practice to attract clients.

Hybrid Model

A hybrid model combines elements of both insurance-based and private-pay approaches. In this model, you will contract with insurance companies while also accepting private-pay clients. Advantages of a hybrid model include

1. Diversified streams of income: By combining insurance and private-pay clients, you can balance the advantages and disadvantages of each model and create a more stable revenue stream.
2. Expanded client base: A hybrid model allows you to serve a broader range of clients, including those with insurance coverage and those who prefer to pay out-of-pocket.
3. Greater flexibility: You can tailor your practice to your preferences, focusing on insurance or private-pay clients as desired.

Disadvantages of a hybrid model include

1. Increased administrative workload: Accepting both private payments and insurance reimbursements can lead to a heavier administrative workload. This is due to the need for more time and effort to bill, track payments, and organize financial records.

2. Unpredictable cash flow: Receiving payments from insurance companies and private-pay clients can lead to a less predictable flow of income since reimbursement from insurance is delayed and is occasionally denied. This can complicate your financial planning and budgeting processes. You will need to review your financial projections regularly to ensure your revenue will be sufficient to meet your income goals and cover your practice's expenses.

—◦◦◦—

When evaluating which payment model to choose for your practice, consider your values, financial goals, and the population you plan to work with.

Remember that your payment model choice is not set in stone. As your practice evolves, you may find that your needs and preferences change, and you can adapt your model accordingly. The key is regularly assessing your financial performance, client satisfaction, and personal and professional well-being to ensure your chosen payment model aligns with your practice's goals and values.

Now that you understand which payment model best aligns with your practice's goals, you're ready to take the next steps in your private practice journey. In the following section, we will explore the process of budgeting for your practice's start-up expenses and ongoing operational costs so you have a solid financial foundation.

BUDGETING FOR START-UP EXPENSES AND ONGOING OPERATIONAL COSTS

Creating a comprehensive budget is one of the most critical aspects of launching and managing a successful private practice. It will serve as a road map for your practice's financial future by helping you allocate resources effectively, plan for growth, and make informed decisions. When developing your budget, it's essential to consider both your start-up costs and ongoing operational expenses.

When launching your private practice, it's important to understand the start-up expenses you'll face. These expenses can vary significantly based on your location, specialty, and business model. To help you plan effectively, here's a breakdown of common start-up costs:

1. **Business Formation and Licensing Fees.** Depending on the business structure you chose in chapter 3, you'll need to pay fees to legally form and register your business at the state level, local level, or both. These fees vary by location, so research the specific requirements for your chosen structure and area to budget accurately.

2. **Office Space.** If you have decided to provide in-person services, you'll need an office space. When looking for office space, remember to budget for monthly rent, security deposit, first and last month's rent, and any necessary renovations. To keep expenses low, consider subleasing by the day or hour. For example, I initially rented from a friend who charged me per client until I filled my caseload, which kept my overhead low.

3. **Office Furniture.** Invest in comfortable and professional office furniture that creates a warm and inviting

space for your clients. This may include items such as a couch, armchairs, side tables, lamps, and other elements that reflect your personal style and therapeutic approach.

4. **Office Technology and Communication Setup.** Budget for essential office equipment such as a computer, printer, work phone line, internet, and HIPAA-compliant email service.

5. **Therapeutic Resources and Tools.** Set aside funds for any specialized therapeutic tools, books, or other resources you'll need based on your clinical approach and clientele.

6. **Malpractice and Liability Insurance.** Research and budget for professional liability insurance to protect against potential legal claims or damages.

7. **Professional Service Fees.** Set aside money for professional services to help you establish a solid legal and financial foundation for your practice. This may include legal fees for reviewing or drafting forms, accounting fees for setting up your bookkeeping system, and consulting fees for business planning.

8. **Marketing and Branding.** Plan to invest in building a solid brand and effectively marketing your practice. This includes costs for buying a domain, designing a professional logo, building a website, printing business cards and marketing materials, and investing in initial advertising such as online directories.

9. **Professional Development and Networking.** Allocate funds for professional membership dues, conference and trainings, and business coaching. Ongoing learning and networking are important investments for your success.

10. **Professional Licenses and Certifications.** Budget for any professional licenses or certifications required to practice legally in your state or specialty. This may include fees for initial licensure, renewals, and continuing education courses necessary to maintain your credentials.

11. **Practice Management Software.** Invest in a reliable practice management software system. For virtual or hybrid practices, ensure it supports secure, HIPAA-compliant telehealth sessions. For any practice model, the software should streamline administrative tasks like scheduling, client communication, and progress note writing.

12. **Accounting/Bookkeeping Software.** Choose accounting or bookkeeping software that simplifies your financial management tasks, such as tracking income and expenses, generating invoices, and preparing tax documents. Factor in the costs of purchasing the software and any ongoing subscription fees.

13. **Emergency Fund/Cash Reserve.** Set aside a reserve of at least three to six months of operating expenses to cover unexpected costs or revenue shortfalls.

It's important to note that not all of these start-up costs will apply to every practice. Your expenses will depend on your business model (e.g., in-person versus virtual services), clinical specialty, and growth plans. As you create your budget, consider which costs are essential for launching and operating your unique practice.

Prioritize the expenses directly contributing to your ability to provide high-quality care and meet your business goals. For example, if you plan to offer primarily virtual services, you may need to allocate more funds for telehealth software and less for physical office space. Or, if you specialize in a niche area, you may need to invest more in targeted marketing and specialized training.

By tailoring your start-up budget to your individual practice needs and goals, you'll be better positioned to allocate your resources effectively and set up your business for long-term success.

After launching your private practice, it's crucial to budget for the ongoing operational expenses to keep your business running smoothly. These costs will vary based on factors such as your location, business model, and individual needs, but here are some common categories to consider:

1. **Office Expenses.** Budget for monthly rent payments, utilities (heat, water, electricity), cleaning services and supplies, repairs and maintenance, furnishings (replacements or additions), and office supplies (paper, pens, printer ink, etc.) to keep your workspace functional and inviting.

2. **Technology and Communication.** Allocate funds for reliable phone and internet services, email service provider, website hosting, and website maintenance to ensure seamless communication with clients and colleagues.

3. **Practice Management System.** Invest in a comprehensive practice management system that includes features such as electronic health records (EHR), teletherapy capabilities, secure messaging, file sharing, and scheduling to streamline your administrative tasks and maintain HIPAA compliance.

4. **Therapeutic Resources and Tools.** Set aside funds for ongoing purchases and subscriptions related to therapeutic resources, such as books, workbooks, assessment

tools, art supplies, and online resources, that support your clinical work and professional development.

5. **Marketing and Advertising.** Plan for ongoing marketing expenses, such as search engine optimization (SEO), online advertising, design services for promotional materials, and directory listings, to promote your practice effectively and attract new clients.

6. **Accounting and Bookkeeping.** Budget for accounting software, monthly accounting and bookkeeping services, and tax preparation to ensure accurate financial management and compliance with tax regulations.

7. **Insurance.** Account for the cost of essential insurance policies, such as professional liability insurance, general liability insurance, and cyber liability insurance, to protect your practice and personal assets.

8. **Billing and Credentialing Services.** If you plan to accept insurance or work with third-party payers, allocate funds for the fees associated with billing and credentialing services to ensure timely and accurate reimbursement.

9. **Professional Development.** Budget for continuing education courses, workshops, conference registration and travel expenses, professional association memberships, and certifications to maintain your licenses and stay current in your field.

10. **Taxes and Fees.** Factor in federal, state, and local income taxes, self-employment taxes, business license renewal fees, professional license renewal fees, and any industry-specific taxes or surcharges to meet your legal obligations and avoid penalties.

11. **Miscellaneous Expenses.** Set aside a small budget for unexpected or infrequent expenses that may arise, such

as replacing a broken piece of equipment or making a charitable donation.

Remember, this list is not exhaustive, and your specific ongoing operational costs will depend on your practice's unique needs and structure. Review your budget regularly and adjust as needed to track and plan for these recurring expenses accurately.

By carefully budgeting for your ongoing operational costs, including therapeutic resources and tools, you'll be better equipped to provide high-quality care to your clients while maintaining a financially sustainable practice. As your practice grows and evolves, make sure to update your budget to reflect any changes in your expenses or revenue streams.

SETTING FEES THAT WILL ALLOW YOU TO PROSPER

Setting the right fees for your services is critical to building a thriving and sustainable private practice. Your fees should reflect the value of your expertise, experience, and the transformative impact you have on your clients' lives. While it's important to be aware of market rates, it's equally crucial to approach fee setting with an abundance mindset and a deep sense of confidence in the value you provide.

Consider taking the following steps when determining your fees:

1. **Conduct market research.** Research the going rates for therapy services in your area, considering factors such as location, specialty, and years of experience. Use this information to understand the range of fees in

your market, but don't feel pressured to set your fees low simply because others do.

2. **Set fees that reflect your value.** Your fees should communicate the value you place on your time, expertise, and the transformative work you do with your clients. Don't underestimate the profound impact you have on your clients' lives and the ripple effect it creates in their relationships, careers, and overall well-being. Set fees that honor the depth and importance of your work, and trust that the right clients will be willing to invest in the value you provide.

3. **Embrace an abundance mindset.** When setting fees, it's essential to approach the process with an abundance mindset rather than a scarcity mindset. A scarcity mindset may lead you to believe that if you set your fees too high, you won't be able to attract enough clients. However, an abundance mindset trusts that there are plenty of clients who are looking for the unique value and expertise you offer and are willing to pay accordingly. Embrace the belief that by setting fees that reflect your worth, you'll attract clients who are deeply committed to their personal growth and value the transformative power of therapy.

4. **Account for your business expenses.** As discussed in the previous section, it's important to consider your overall business expenses when determining your fees. You want to ensure that your fees are sufficient to cover your expenses, support your practice's financial well-being, and allow for reinvestment in your professional growth and development.

5. **Evaluate your personal expenses and financial goals.** Before determining your fees, it's crucial to clearly understand your personal financial needs and

long-term goals. Create a detailed monthly budget that includes all your living expenses, such as housing, food, transportation, health care, and savings. This will give you a clear picture of the income you need to generate from your practice to support your desired lifestyle and future aspirations.

6. **Consider vacation time and client load.** When setting your fees, it's important to factor in the amount of vacation time you want to take each year and the number of clients you feel comfortable seeing per week. Determine the number of weeks you'd like to take off annually for rest, rejuvenation, and professional development. Additionally, consider the ideal number of clients you want to see each week to maintain a healthy work-life balance and prevent burnout. These factors will impact your overall income and should be accounted for when calculating your fees.

7. **Plan for taxes.** As a self-employed therapist, it's crucial to remember that a portion of your income will need to be set aside for taxes. Consult with a financial professional or accountant to determine the appropriate percentage to allocate for taxes based on your income and business structure. By factoring in taxes from the outset, you can set fees that ensure you're meeting your financial obligations while still allowing for a prosperous income.

For example, let's say you've determined that your desired monthly net income is $8,500, and your monthly business expenses are $1,500. You want to take four weeks off per year and feel comfortable seeing twenty clients per week. Your tax rate is estimated at 30 percent. Here's how you can calculate your fee per session:

Step 1: Calculate the annual net income needed.

To calculate your desired annual net income, use this formula:

Monthly net income x 12 months = Annual net income
In this case: $8,500 × 12 months = $102,000

Step 2: Calculate the annual gross income needed (i.e., before taxes and expenses).

To account for taxes, divide your desired annual net income by (1 minus your tax rate). This calculation ensures you determine the total gross income required before taxes are deducted.

Formula: Annual net income ÷ (1 - Tax rate) = Annual gross income
Example: $102,000 ÷ (1 − 0.30) = $145,714

Step 3: Calculate the total annual business expenses.

To determine your total annual business expenses, multiple your total monthly expenses by twelve months. This gives you the full cost of running your practice for the year.

Formula: Monthly business expenses x 12 = Annual business expenses
Example: $1,500 × 12 months = $18,000

Step 4: Calculate the total annual gross income needed (including business expenses).

To determine the total gross income needed, add your annual gross income (before taxes) to your total annual business expenses. This ensures that you account for your personal income needs and the cost of running your practice.

Formula: Annual gross income + Annual business
expenses = Total annual gross income
Example: $145,714 + $18,000 = $163,714

Step 5: Determine the number of weeks worked per year.

To calculate the number of weeks you'll work in a year, subtract the number of weeks you plan to take off from the total number of weeks in a year. This accounts for vacation or personal time.

Formula: Total weeks in a year – Weeks off = Weeks
worked per year
Example: 52 weeks – 4 weeks off = 48 weeks

Step 6: Calculate the total number of sessions per year.

To determine the total number of sessions you'll conduct in a year, multiply the number of clients you plan to see each week by the number of weeks you'll work in a year.

Formula: Clients per week x Weeks worked per year =
Total sessions per year
Example: 20 clients per week × 48 weeks = 960 sessions

Step 7: Calculate the fee per session.

To calculate the fee you need to charge per session, divide your total annual gross income by the total number of sessions you'll conduct in a year. This gives you the minimum fee required to meet your income and expenses goals.

Formula: Total annual gross income ÷ Total sessions per
year = Fee per session
Example: $163,714 ÷ 960 sessions = $171 per session
(rounded to the nearest dollar)

In this scenario, following the calculations outlined above, the therapist would need to set their fee at a minimum of $171 per session to achieve a monthly net income of $8,500, cover monthly business expenses of $1,500, set aside 30 percent for taxes, and take four weeks off per year while seeing twenty clients per week. For simplicity, this fee can be rounded up to $175 per session.

—∞∞∞—

Remember, your fees are a reflection of the value you place on your expertise, your time, and the transformative work you do. By setting fees that align with your worth and approaching the process with an abundance mindset, you'll create a thriving practice that supports your financial well-being and allows you to make a profound impact in your clients' lives.

When discussing fees with potential clients, focus on communicating the value and transformative impact of your services. Help clients understand that investing in therapy is an investment in their personal growth, relationships, and overall quality of life. By confidently articulating the value you provide, you'll attract clients who are committed to their well-being and are willing to prioritize their mental health.

Trust in the unique value you bring to your work, and have faith that the right clients will be drawn to your practice, ready to invest in their growth and healing. By setting fees that honor your worth, you're not only paving the way for your own prosperity but also attracting clients who are deeply committed to their personal transformation.

STREAMLINING FEE COLLECTION WITH HIPAA-COMPLIANT STRATEGIES

Implementing efficient and HIPAA-compliant fee-collection strategies is essential for maintaining a steady cash flow and protecting client privacy. When selecting a payment processing system, ensure the provider is HIPAA-compliant and agrees to sign a Business Associate Agreement (BAA) with your practice. Here are some best practices to consider:

1. **Use an integrated payment processor.** Select a payment processor integrated with your HIPAA-compliant electronic health record (EHR) or practice management system. This integration allows you to easily generate invoices, process payments, and keep track of outstanding balances while ensuring all transactions are secure and compliant with HIPAA regulations.

2. **Consider standalone HIPAA-compliant payment apps:** If your EHR or practice management system does not have an integrated payment processor, consider using a standalone HIPAA-compliant payment app like Ivy Pay. Ivy Pay is designed specifically for therapists and will sign a BAA with your practice to ensure HIPAA compliance.

3. **Offer HIPAA-compliant payment options**. Offer payment options that are HIPAA compliant, such as credit or debit cards processed through your EHR's integrated payment system or Ivy Pay, HSA/FSA cards, and ACH bank transfers. Avoid using popular payment apps like Venmo, PayPal, Zelle, and Apple Pay, as they are not HIPAA compliant.

4. **Secure handling of cash or checks.** If accepting cash or checks, ensure you have secure, HIPAA-compliant

methods for storing and documenting these transactions, such as a locked cash box and a secure electronic record-keeping system.

5. **Establish clear payment policies**. Clearly communicate your payment policies to clients up front, including session fees, cancellation policies, and payment due dates. Obtain written consent from clients to store and process their payment information securely, ensuring your systems meet HIPAA requirements for data privacy and security.

6. **Automate payment reminders and follow-up messages**. Utilize the features of your EHR or practice management system to automate payment reminders and follow-up messages. This reduces the time spent on collections and minimizes the risk of late or missed payments.

By implementing these strategies and prioritizing HIPAA compliance, you'll create a seamless and secure fee-collection process that supports your practice's financial health while safeguarding client confidentiality and trust. Remember to review and update your payment processing systems regularly to ensure ongoing compliance with HIPAA regulations and industry best practices.

NAVIGATING THE INSURANCE CREDENTIALING PROCESS

For therapists who choose to accept insurance, getting credentialed with insurance panels is a crucial step in building a sustainable practice. The credentialing process involves submitting applications, providing documentation, and following up with insurance companies to become an in-network provider. Here are the key steps in the credentialing process and the options available for therapists:

1. Research the insurance plans that are most commonly used by your target client population, and gather information on their credentialing requirements and application processes.
2. Prepare your credentialing materials, including your license, malpractice insurance, NPI number, and any specialties or certifications.
3. Complete the credentialing applications thoroughly and accurately, following each insurance panel's specific guidelines and deadlines.
4. Be prepared for a lengthy process, as credentialing can take several months to complete. Plan your practice's cash flow and marketing strategies accordingly.
5. Follow up regularly with insurance panels to check the status of your application and provide any additional information or documentation as needed.
6. Once credentialed, familiarize yourself with each insurance panel's policies, fee schedules, and billing procedures to ensure smooth claims processing and reimbursement.

Therapists have three main options when navigating the credentialing process:

1. **Navigating the process independently.** This option provides the most control but can be time-consuming and requires a significant amount of administrative work.
2. **Working with a credentialing company.** These companies specialize in supporting mental health

90

professionals with insurance credentialing and contracting. They can save time and reduce administrative burden but come with additional costs.
3. **Partnering with a comprehensive support company.** Some companies offer a wide range of services, including assistance with credentialing, billing, and practice management. They provide expertise in navigating insurance requirements and maximizing reimbursements but also may come with additional costs and may require giving up some control over certain aspects of your practice.

Once credentialed, therapists have the option to handle insurance billing themselves or hire a biller. Hiring a biller can save time and reduce the administrative burden of submitting claims, following up on denials, and managing the billing process. However, it also comes with additional costs and may require giving up some control over the billing aspect of your practice.

Pros of hiring a biller:

- Saves time and reduces administrative workload
- Offers expertise in submitting clean claims and maximizing reimbursements
- Stays up-to-date with changing insurance requirements and billing procedures

Cons of hiring a biller:

- Additional costs for billing services
- Less direct control over the billing process
- Potential for communication gaps or delays between the biller and the therapist

When deciding whether or not to hire a biller, consider your comfort level with billing tasks, the amount of time you can dedicate to billing, your budget for outsourcing these services, and your desired level of control over your practice's billing operations.

By understanding the credentialing process, exploring your options, and making informed decisions about billing, you can set up your practice for long-term success and sustainability while providing excellent care to your clients.

PARTNERING WITH FINANCIAL PROFESSIONALS TO STRENGTHEN YOUR PRACTICE

As you establish and grow your private practice, seeking guidance from financial professionals can help you make informed decisions, optimize your finances, and plan for long-term success. Here are some key questions to ask when working with accountants and financial advisors:

1. What experience do you have working with therapy practices or small businesses in the health care industry?
2. How can you help me structure my practice to maximize tax benefits and minimize financial risks?
3. What strategies can you recommend for tracking my practice's financial performance and making data-driven decisions?
4. How can you support me in developing a long-term financial plan that aligns with my personal and professional goals?
5. What should I be aware of when it comes to tax deductions, estimated tax payments, and other tax-related issues specific to therapy practices?

6. Can you provide guidance on retirement planning and saving for the future as a self-employed therapist?
7. How often should we review my practice's financial health and adjust my financial strategies as needed?

Remember, building a relationship with a trusted accountant or financial advisor can provide invaluable support as you navigate the financial aspects of running a successful practice. Look for professionals who understand the unique challenges and opportunities of the therapy industry and who can offer tailored guidance to help you thrive.

MASTERING THE BASICS OF BOOKKEEPING AND FINANCIAL TRACKING

Effective bookkeeping and financial tracking are essential for maintaining the financial health of your practice and making informed business decisions. As a practice owner, it's important to understand these processes, even if you choose to work with a bookkeeper or accountant. Here are some key elements to consider:

1. **Implement a bookkeeping system.** Use accounting software like QuickBooks or Xero to record your practice's financial transactions, including income, expenses, and payments. Consistently categorize your transactions to make generating financial reports and preparing for tax filing easier.
2. **Track your income.** Keep detailed records of all income sources, including client payments, insurance reimbursements, and other revenue streams, through your EHR system. Utilize its built-in invoicing features to generate and send professional invoices, process

payments securely, and track outstanding balances. If possible, set up automated reminders within your EHR to follow up on any unpaid invoices, ensuring timely payments and maintaining financial stability in your practice.

3. **Monitor your expenses.** Record all business-related expenses, including rent, utilities, supplies, marketing, and professional development. Keep receipts and documentation for each expense to ensure accurate record-keeping and maximize tax deductions.

4. **Reconcile your accounts.** Regularly compare your bookkeeping records against your bank and credit card statements to identify discrepancies or errors. This process helps you maintain accurate financial records and detect potential issues early on.

5. **Generate financial reports.** Use your bookkeeping software to create key financial reports, such as profit and loss statements, balance sheets, and cash flow statements. Review these reports regularly to assess your practice's financial performance and make data-driven decisions.

6. **Establish a system for financial review.** Set aside time each month or quarter to review your financial records, assess your progress toward your financial goals, and make any necessary adjustments to your budget or financial strategies.

By mastering the basics of bookkeeping and financial tracking, you'll better understand your practice's financial health and be better equipped to make informed decisions that support your long-term success. Remember, investing time in developing your financial management skills is an investment in the sustainability and growth of your practice.

REFLECT AND TAKE ACTION

Congratulations on completing this chapter on building a financially empowered practice! Throughout this chapter, you've gained valuable insights and strategies for choosing the right payment model, setting aligned fees, budgeting for start-up and ongoing expenses, navigating insurance credentialing, and mastering basic bookkeeping.

Key Takeaways

- Choosing the right payment model for your practice involves carefully considering your target population, financial goals, and personal preferences and being open to adapting your approach as your practice evolves.
- Setting fees that reflect the value of your expertise and the transformative impact of your work is crucial for attracting clients who are invested in their growth and creating a sustainable, fulfilling practice.
- Carefully budgeting for start-up costs and ongoing expenses while considering your unique business model and needs helps you allocate resources effectively and make informed financial decisions.
- Navigating insurance credentialing involves understanding your options, such as working independently, partnering with a credentialing company, or utilizing a comprehensive support service, and being prepared for the time and effort required to complete the process successfully.
- Implementing efficient, HIPAA-compliant fee-collection strategies and considering the pros and cons of hiring a biller is essential for maintaining a steady cash flow and protecting client privacy.

- Developing a basic understanding of bookkeeping, financial tracking, and goal setting empowers you to take control of your practice's financial health and make data-driven decisions that support your long-term vision.

Action Steps

1. Evaluate the payment models available and decide which approach best aligns with your practice goals and values. If you're unsure, consider contacting colleagues or mentors for guidance and insights.
2. Develop a fee structure that reflects your value and expertise as a therapist. If you feel resistance or discomfort around setting your fees, use this as an opportunity to explore and challenge any limiting beliefs holding you back.
3. Create a comprehensive budget for your practice that accounts for both start-up costs and ongoing expenses. Be sure to include often-overlooked items such as self-care, retirement savings, and professional development.
4. If you plan to accept insurance, research the credentialing process and requirements for the panels you're interested in. Decide whether you'll navigate the process independently or seek support from a credentialing company or comprehensive support service.
5. Research and implement HIPAA-compliant fee-collection strategies that streamline your billing process and protect client privacy. Consider the pros and cons of hiring a biller to manage your insurance claims and revenue cycle.
6. Commit to implementing a basic bookkeeping system, and schedule regular financial tracking and review time. Use this data to assess your progress toward your

goals and make informed decisions about your practice's growth and development.

Remember, building a financially empowered practice is an ongoing journey that requires patience, perseverance, and a willingness to learn and grow. By consistently applying the principles and strategies outlined in this chapter, you'll set yourself up for long-term success and sustainability.

Trust in your unique value as a therapist, and believe in your ability to create a thriving practice that makes a lasting difference in your clients' lives. Embrace the challenges and opportunities that arise, knowing that each step you take toward financial empowerment is a step toward building the practice and life of your dreams. You've got this!

6

CREATING MAGNETIC MESSAGING TO ATTRACT YOUR IDEAL CLIENTS

Your messaging is the foundation of your marketing strategy and is crucial for attracting your ideal clients to your practice. It is the starting point that grabs the attention of potential clients and conveys who you are, what you offer, and why they should choose you.

Developing the right message allows you to form a deeper connection with your ideal clients. Effective messaging builds understanding and trust, which is essential for creating a solid therapeutic relationship. By using language that acknowledges their experiences, speaks to their pain points, and presents a clear pathway to transformation, you show that you truly comprehend their needs and have the ability to support them on their journey.

To create client-centered messages, you need a thorough understanding of your niche and ideal client profile. Understanding who you serve enables you to adapt your language, tone, and content to align with their unique needs and aspirations. Well-crafted messaging has the power to draw in your ideal clients and establish meaningful relationships built on trust and loyalty.

In this chapter, we will discuss the process of creating impactful, client-centered messages that resonate with your target audience. We will discuss key principles to ensure your communication is clear, empathetic, consistent, and authentic. By the end, you will have the knowledge and tools to craft a compelling core message that encapsulates your unique value proposition and speaks directly to the needs and desires of your ideal clients, guiding all aspects of your marketing efforts. Your messaging will become the north star that attracts the clients you are meant to serve and helps you build a thriving practice.

USING THE POWER OF MESSAGING TO CONNECT WITH YOUR IDEAL CLIENT

Messaging is the foundation of effective marketing. It's how you communicate the core of your practice, your unique value, and the transformative benefits you provide to potential clients. It's the specific language, tone, and content you use to convey who you are, what you offer, and how you can help your ideal clients achieve their desired outcomes.

When your messaging deeply connects with your ideal clients, it captivates and engages them from the first interaction. By crafting messages that acknowledge your clients' struggles, address their pain points, and paint a vivid picture of the transformation they seek, you demonstrate a deep understanding of their unique experiences. This level of empathy and authenticity sets the stage for a meaningful therapeutic relationship, where clients feel seen, heard, and supported from the beginning.

When your messages clearly articulate your unique approach and the transformative benefits you offer, potential clients are more likely to choose you as their guide. Consistent and compelling messaging builds trust, credibility, and professionalism. It's the first point of connection that conveys your expertise and inspires potential clients to take the next step in working with you.

Combining a deep understanding of your clients with authenticity in your messaging creates a magnetic pull that draws in clients who are the perfect fit for your practice. This establishes meaningful therapeutic relationships and builds a thriving practice that significantly changes both your clients' lives and your own.

APPLYING THE KEY PRINCIPLES OF EFFECTIVE MESSAGING

By incorporating the principles of clarity, empathy, consistency, and authenticity into your messaging, you can create a powerful connection that draws your ideal clients to your services. Let's explore each of these principles in more detail.

Clarity

Clarity is crucial because it ensures your ideal clients understand exactly how your services can help them overcome their challenges and achieve their desired outcomes. When your message is clear and focused on their needs, potential clients are more likely to engage with you and see you as the solution they've been seeking.

Here are three ways to achieve clarity in your messaging:

- Use language that reflects your clients' experiences and resonates with their needs.
- Clearly articulate the specific challenges you will help them overcome and the transformations they can expect.

- Provide a clear call to action that guides them toward the next step in their journey with you.

Here's what clear messaging sounds like: "Anxiety can make everyday life feel overwhelming, but support is available. Through personalized therapy, I help clients break free from constant worry and find a greater sense of peace. Schedule a free consultation to start your journey toward healing."

Empathy

Empathy is a cornerstone of effective messaging. By demonstrating a deep understanding and compassion for your clients' struggles, you build trust and show that you are a true partner in their journey toward healing and growth.

Here are three ways to incorporate empathy into your messaging:

1. Validate their experiences and emotions using language that resonates with their unique challenges.
2. Share relatable stories or testimonials that showcase how you've helped others in similar situations.
3. Use a warm, compassionate tone that conveys your genuine care and commitment to their well-being.

Here's what empathetic messaging sounds like: "I know how overwhelming life can be, and I've walked alongside many people facing similar struggles. You don't have to figure it all out alone. With support and understanding, healing is possible. I'm here to help you take that first step."

Consistency

Consistency in your messaging reinforces your unique brand and approach, building trust and familiarity with your ideal clients. When your message consistently reflects their needs and desires across all touchpoints, it creates a cohesive and compelling narrative that draws them to your practice.

To maintain consistency in your messaging, do these three things:

1. Develop a clear brand voice and messaging framework centered on your clients' needs and aspirations.
2. Ensure all your marketing materials, from your website to your social media, consistently reflect your approach.
3. Regularly review and refine your messaging to maintain alignment with your evolving understanding of your clients' needs.

Here's an example of how consistency can be applied across platforms, in this case, on your website and in social media posts:

Website: "At [Your Practice], we specialize in helping ambitious professionals overcome anxiety and self-doubt through our tailored, evidence-based approach. Our compassionate guidance empowers you to build resilience, find balance, and unlock your full potential."

Social Media: "Struggling with anxiety and self-doubt? Our evidence-based approach, tailored to the unique needs of ambitious professionals, helps you build resilience, find balance, and unlock your full potential. Experience the transformative power of compassionate guidance at [Your Practice]."

Authenticity

Authenticity is a critical component of effective messaging for therapists. When your message is grounded in your genuine passion for helping others and your professional experience, it resonates with potential clients and establishes you as a trustworthy and knowledgeable resource.

Incorporating authenticity into your messaging can be as simple as doing the following:

1. Share your professional journey and what inspired you to become a therapist in a way that showcases your dedication to each client's well-being.
2. Highlight the therapeutic approaches and values that guide your work and align with your clients' needs.
3. Express empathy and understanding for the challenges your clients face while maintaining appropriate boundaries.
4. Use a warm and approachable tone that reflects your commitment to creating a safe and supportive therapeutic environment.

Here's an example of authentic messaging: "As a therapist with extensive experience in cognitive-behavioral therapy, I am passionate about helping individuals overcome anxiety and build resilience. I understand the courage it takes to seek support, and I am dedicated to providing a nonjudgmental space where you can explore your thoughts, feelings, and experiences."

By infusing your messaging with clarity, empathy, consistency, and authenticity, you create a powerful connection with potential clients. It reflects your expertise, understanding, and commitment to their well-being, positioning you as a trusted partner in their healing journey and paving the way for a meaningful and impactful therapeutic relationship.

UNDERSTANDING YOUR IDEAL CLIENT

To craft messages that truly connect with your ideal clients, you need to develop a deep understanding of who they are, what they're struggling with, and what they desire most. This involves creating a detailed client profile that goes beyond surface-level demographics to capture the essence of their experiences, challenges, and aspirations.

Defining Your Ideal Client

Your ideal client is the person or group of people who are the perfect fit for your unique services, approach, and values. They are the ones who will benefit most from your expertise and are most likely to form a strong, lasting connection with you. Having a clear picture of your ideal client is essential for developing messaging that speaks directly to their hearts and needs.

Identifying Key Characteristics of Your Ideal Client

To gain a comprehensive understanding of your ideal client, it's important to consider various aspects of their identity, experiences, and goals. Let's explore the key characteristics to focus on.

Demographics:
- Age range, gender, marital status, occupation
- Geographic location and cultural background
- Education level and socioeconomic status

Psychographics:
- Personality traits, values, and beliefs
- Interests, hobbies, and lifestyle preferences
- Communication style and decision-making process

Challenges and Pain Points:
- Specific struggles and obstacles they face
- Emotional and psychological barriers to well-being
- Root causes and triggers of their distress

Desires and Aspirations:
- Ultimate outcomes they wish to achieve through therapy
- Short-term and long-term goals for personal growth
- Vision of their ideal life and relationships

By digging deep into these areas, you can create a vivid, multidimensional profile of your ideal client that captures their unique experiences, needs, and desires. This understanding is the foundation of your messaging, enabling you to create content that deeply connects with your audience and fosters an immediate sense of trust and rapport.

Below is an example of an ideal client profile for a therapist specializing in anxiety.

Demographics: Professional women aged 25–40 living in urban areas

Psychographics: High-achievers, perfectionists, value career and personal growth

Challenges: Overwhelmed by work-life balance, self-doubt, fear of failure

Desires: To find peace, confidence, and fulfillment in their professional and personal lives

With this level of depth and specificity, you can develop messaging that validates your ideal client's struggles, affirms their worth, and offers a clear path to the transformations they seek.

Crafting Messaging Based on Your Ideal Client Profile

Once you clearly understand your ideal client, use this knowledge to infuse every aspect of your messaging with empathy, relevance, and value. Here are some key ways to ensure your messaging aligns with your ideal client profile:

- Mirror the language and phrases they use to describe their challenges and desires.
- Validate their experiences and emotions, showing that you understand their unique struggles.
- Paint a vivid picture of the transformations and outcomes they can achieve through your services.
- Highlight the specific ways your approach and expertise are tailored to their needs.
- Share relatable stories and examples that demonstrate your track record of helping similar clients succeed.
- Offer a clear, compelling call to action that guides them toward the next step in their journey with you.

Here is an example of messaging for the ideal client profile described above:

As a high-achieving woman, you've worked tirelessly to build a successful career and life. But behind the accomplishments, you're struggling with overwhelming anxiety, self-doubt, and the constant fear of not being enough.

I understand how exhausting it can be to keep pushing through while secretly feeling like you're on the verge of burnout. That's why I specialize in helping ambitious women like you find the inner peace, confidence, and balance you deserve.

Through my tailored approach, combining evidence-based techniques and a deep understanding of the unique pressures you face, we'll work together to break free from anxiety's grip and create a life that truly fulfills you.

You don't have to do this alone. Schedule your free consultation today and take the first step toward the joy and ease you've longed for.

Developing a deep understanding of your ideal client is essential for creating effective messaging. By letting this knowledge guide every aspect of your communication, you can craft content that truly resonates with your target audience, fostering trust and positioning you as the ideal therapist to support them on their journey.

This in-depth understanding of your ideal client is the foundation for applying the key principles of effective messaging: clarity, empathy, consistency, and authenticity. When your messages are rooted in a genuine understanding of your target audience, they become a powerful tool for attracting the clients you are most passionate about serving. This sets the stage for building meaningful therapeutic relationships and facilitating transformative change in your clients' lives.

DEVELOPING YOUR CORE MESSAGE

Building upon the deep understanding of your ideal client, your core message is the heart of all your marketing efforts.

It should clearly articulate why clients should choose your practice, focusing on the unique value and transformation you offer through your approach.

Your core message is the culmination of effective messaging principles and your deep understanding of your target audience. It creates a powerful statement that directly addresses their needs and speaks to their emotions.

Here are some steps you can take as you develop your core message:

1. Identify Your Unique Strengths in Serving Your Ideal Client

Your unique strengths form the foundation of your core message. They set you apart from other therapists and showcase your value to your ideal clients. To identify your unique strengths, consider the following:

- Specialized training, certifications, and expertise relevant to your ideal client's needs
- Therapeutic modalities and techniques that align with your target audience's needs
- Personal qualities, values, and experiences that shape your empathetic approach

Here's an example of how to craft those strengths into a messaging statement: "With extensive training in emotionally focused therapy (EFT) and a deep understanding of attachment, I create a safe, nonjudgmental space for couples to explore their unique challenges, strengthen their bond, and rediscover the joy and intimacy they deserve."

2. Define Your Value Proposition

Your value proposition is a powerful statement that communicates the unique value and transformative benefits your ideal clients can expect from working with you. Here are some strategies to use to craft a compelling value proposition:

- Highlight the specific outcomes and transformations your ideal clients desire most.
- Emphasize how your unique strengths and approach address their core struggles and aspirations.
- Use empathetic language that emotionally connects with their experiences and needs.
- Differentiate yourself by showcasing the advantages of your practice.

Here's an example of a value proposition: "I provide a nurturing, play-based therapeutic environment where children can safely express their emotions, develop coping skills, and strengthen their bonds with caregivers. Through an approach tailored to each family's unique needs, I help you navigate challenges, improve communication, and foster your child's resilience and well-being."

3. Write a Core Message with Language That Will Resonate with Your Ideal Client

Your core message should encapsulate the essence of your value proposition, showcasing how you can guide your ideal clients from where they are now to where they want to be. Your core message has three main parts:

1. Headline—A powerful statement that captures your ideal client's attention and communicates the core transformation you offer.

2. Supporting Statements—Specific details that reinforce your headline, highlighting your unique strengths, approach, and the outcomes they can expect.
3. Call to Action—A clear, compelling directive encouraging potential clients to take the next step in their journey with you.

In the following example, notice the attention-grabbing headline, supporting statements, and call to action.

Rediscover Your Inner Strength: Compassionate Therapy for Lasting Transformation

I specialize in empowering individuals like you to overcome anxiety, depression, and trauma through a tailored, trauma-informed approach. With deep empathy and evidence-based techniques, I provide a safe space for you to heal, grow, and reclaim the joyful, fulfilling life you deserve.

You don't have to face your struggles alone. Schedule your free consultation today and take the first step toward unlocking your inner resilience and creating the life you've always envisioned.

Now, let's take that core message to a new level.

For your core message to build a stronger connection between you and your ideal client, it's important for that person to "recognize" themselves, their felt needs, challenges, and desired outcomes, in your message. You want them to feel seen, heard, and understood and to recognize that you are the right guide to support them in overcoming their struggles and achieving the transformation they desire.

This can be achieved by

- using the same kind of language your ideal clients use to describe their experiences, struggles, and aspirations;
- validating their pain points and offering solutions that directly address their unique challenges and goal; and
- infusing your message with empathy, understanding, and commitment to their healing journey.

Begin by making a list of words your ideal client might use to describe the pain they feel today and a second list of words they might use to describe how they wish they could feel. Crafting a core message that promises to help them get from where they are today to where they long to be lets them know you "get them" and builds connection and trust.

Here's an example of a core message that incorporates the kind of language that may feel familiar to someone who is struggling:

Feeling anxious? Overwhelmed? Isolated?

Peace, confidence, and joy might feel out of reach—but they're not. I've helped countless women on their healing journeys, and I can help you too. I offer a compassionate, judgment-free space where, together, we will develop personalized strategies to help you unlock your inner resilience and create the life you've always envisioned. With my specialized training in evidence-based techniques and a deep commitment to your unique needs, I'll guide you every step of the way.

Your journey to healing and empowerment begins now. Schedule your free consultation today.

MAINTAINING CONSISTENCY ACROSS PLATFORMS

Once you've developed your core message, it's crucial to maintain consistency across all your marketing channels. Consistency reinforces your brand identity, builds trust, and ensures your unique value proposition resonates with your ideal clients, regardless of where they encounter your message. This is an extension of the principle of consistency discussed earlier, applied to your core message.

Here are a few reminders as you adapt your core message for different platforms while maintaining consistency:

- Preserve the essence of your value proposition, tone, and key benefits across all channels.
- Tailor the language and format to suit the specific constraints and best practices of each platform (e.g., character limits on social media, visual elements in print materials).
- Ensure your message always leads with empathy, understanding, and a clear focus on your clients' needs and desired outcomes.

Here are examples of how to communicate the same core message across various platforms:

Website home page: "Welcome, I'm so glad you're here. If you're struggling with anxiety, self-doubt, or feeling overwhelmed by life's challenges, I want you to know that you're not alone. My compassionate, evidence-based approach is designed to help you develop the tools and resilience you need to reclaim your joy, confidence, and inner peace. Through our work together, tailored to your unique needs and goals, you'll discover the strength within to overcome any obstacle and create the life you truly desire. I invite you to schedule a free consultation today – your journey to healing and empowerment starts now."

Social media post: "You deserve to break free from the constant worry and self-doubt holding you back from the joyful, fulfilling life you envision. I'm here to guide you every step of the way with compassionate support and proven strategies tailored to your unique needs. Let's unlock your inner resilience together— schedule your free consultation today and take the first step toward transformative change."

Third person version for an ad or bio: "Jane Smith helps women unlock their inner resilience, overcome anxiety, and heal from self-doubt. Her compassion and strategies have helped many rediscover joy, confidence, and inner peace as they embrace the life they desire. The journey to healing and empowerment begins with a free consultation. Call or email today."

By infusing every touchpoint with your core message, you create a cohesive, resonant brand experience that draws your ideal clients to your practice. They'll feel understood, supported, and empowered to take the next step in their healing journey with you as their trusted guide.

Developing a powerful core message is the natural progression from understanding your ideal client and embracing the principles of effective messaging. By combining clarity, empathy, consistency, and authenticity with your deep knowledge of your target audience, you create a message that truly resonates and positions you as the perfect guide for their transformative journey.

BRINGING IT ALL TOGETHER

Crafting magnetic messaging is at the core of your therapy practice's marketing strategy.

By deeply understanding your ideal clients, articulating your unique value proposition, and infusing your messaging with clarity, empathy, consistency, and authenticity, you create a powerful foundation for attracting and connecting with the clients you're meant to serve.

As you continue on your private practice journey, remember that developing effective messaging is an ongoing process. Continuously refine and adapt your messaging based on market trends, performance data, and your own experiences to ensure it remains relevant, impactful, and aligned with your evolving brand.

REFLECT AND TAKE ACTION

Before you begin creating your marketing materials and online presence, take a moment to reflect on the key takeaways from this chapter.

Key Takeaways
- Messaging serves as the cornerstone of effective marketing by helping you communicate the essence of your practice, your unique value proposition, and the transformative benefits you offer to your ideal clients.
- Resonant and authentic messaging captivates and engages your ideal clients, fosters meaningful

therapeutic relationships, and helps you stand out in a crowded market.

- Incorporating the principles of clarity, empathy, consistency, and authenticity in your messaging creates a powerful connection with your ideal clients and positions you as a trusted partner in their healing journey.
- Developing a deep understanding of your ideal client involves creating a detailed profile that captures their demographics, psychographics, challenges and pain points, as well as their desires and aspirations.
- Crafting messaging based on your ideal client profile involves mirroring their language, validating their experiences, painting a vivid picture of the transformations they can achieve, and offering a clear call to action.
- Your core messaging should reflect your unique strengths, define your value proposition, and include a powerful statement that encapsulates the essence of the transformation you offer.
- Ensuring alignment between your clients' needs and your language in messaging requires reflecting on the words your ideal clients use, validating their pain points, and infusing your message with empathy and understanding.
- Maintaining consistency across platforms is crucial; preserve the essence of your value proposition, tailor the language to suit each platform, and always lead with empathy while focusing on your clients' needs and desired outcomes.

Action Steps

1. Develop a comprehensive ideal client profile that includes their demographics, psychographics,

challenges, and desires. Use this as a guidepost for all your messaging decisions.

2. Identify your unique strengths as a therapist and the specific transformations you help clients achieve. Incorporate these elements into your core message and value proposition.

3. Craft your core message framework, including a compelling headline, supporting statements, and a clear call to action. Ensure your message is authentic, empathetic, and consistent with your brand voice.

By following these action steps and remaining committed to refining your messaging, you'll create a strong foundation for attracting and connecting with your ideal clients as you build your thriving therapy practice.

As you move forward, keep your ideal clients at the heart of every messaging decision. By staying true to your authentic voice and committing to their transformation, you'll create a strong foundation for your marketing efforts and be well-prepared to connect with the clients who need your unique support the most.

In the next chapter, we'll explore how to amplify your online presence and leverage your magnetic messaging to reach and attract your ideal clients through your online presence. With a strong messaging foundation in place, you'll be ready to build a thriving therapy practice that makes a meaningful difference in the lives of those you serve.

7

EFFECTIVE MARKETING STRATEGIES TO ATTRACT YOUR IDEAL CLIENTS

Having a compelling message that speaks directly to the needs of your ideal clients is only part of the equation. To truly connect with those you're meant to serve, you must master the art of getting that message in front of the right audience through effective marketing strategies.

As a therapist, your expertise and insight have the power to transform lives profoundly. However, in today's crowded therapy landscape, simply being exceptional at what you do is no longer enough. You must harness the power of marketing to bridge the gap between your unique offerings and the individuals who need your support the most.

Marketing allows you to amplify your authentic voice and attract ideal clients to your practice. It's about creating an online presence that captures who you are and what you offer in a way that deeply resonates with your target audience.

This chapter will show you how to build that powerful marketing engine through strategies like developing an authentic brand identity, crafting a client-attracting website, optimizing for search visibility, and leveraging tools like Google Business Profile. Each component is designed to help you get your message out there and connect with an abundance of clients you're passionate about serving.

If you're ready to take your practice to new heights and make a more significant impact through smart marketing, let's dive in—starting with the critical first step of defining a strong brand identity.

DEVELOPING A STRONG BRAND IDENTITY

Imagine you're scrolling through social media, looking for fitness inspiration. You come across a personal trainer's post that catches your eye. The images showcase their clients' incredible transformations, while the captions share valuable tips and insights. Intrigued, you visit their profile and find a cohesive theme, engaging content, and a link to their website. On their site, every element—from the colors and font to the language and imagery—reinforces a message of dedication, expertise, and empowerment. This is the significance of a strong personal brand.

Your brand is the essence of your practice—it's the promise you make to your clients, the values you stand for, and the personality you convey in every interaction. In a crowded market, a well-defined brand identity helps you stand out, build trust, and attract the right clients.

Think of your favorite brands—the ones you trust and admire. These brands have a strong, cohesive identity that resonates with you on a personal level. The same principles apply to your therapy practice. A strong brand identity

- sets you apart from competitors and showcases what makes you unique,
- builds trust and credibility and conveys expertise and reliability,

- creates a memorable presence and makes your practice recognizable and memorable, and
- attracts your ideal clients and aligns with your ideal client's values, preferences, and needs.

As you develop your brand identity, staying true to yourself and your practice is crucial. Authenticity is key—your brand should reflect your genuine personality, values, and approach to therapy. Clients can sense inauthenticity, which erodes trust.

Reflect on what makes you unique as a therapist. Consider the following about yourself:

- Personality traits—warm and nurturing or direct and action oriented?
- Communication style—casual and conversational or formal and professional?
- Values and beliefs—what principles guide your work?
- Specialties and approach—what makes your therapeutic style unique?

By staying true to yourself, you'll create a brand identity that feels natural, genuine, and attractive to the right clients.

The Building Blocks of Your Brand

Visual Identity. Your visual identity includes all the graphical elements that represent your brand, such as your logo, color palette, fonts, and imagery. These elements should work together to create a cohesive, visually appealing presence that reflects your practice's personality and values.

When designing your visual identity, consider the following:

- **Color psychology.** Different colors evoke different emotions. Choose colors that align with your brand personality and the feelings you want to convey.
- **Typography.** Your font choices should be legible, professional, and reflective of your brand personality.
- **Imagery.** Use high-quality, relevant photos and graphics that resonate with your target audience.

Voice and Messaging. Your brand voice and messaging encompass the language, tone, and key messages you use to communicate with your audience. Develop a consistent voice that aligns with your brand personality and resonates with your ideal clients.

Consider these components:

- Tone—Warm and empathetic or straightforward and professional? Balance authenticity and appropriateness.
- Language—Use clear, accessible language that your clients will understand.
- Key messages—Identify the core messages about your practice, such as your unique approach, the benefits of working with you, and the transformations your clients can expect.

Values and Personality. Your brand values are the guiding principles that shape your practice and your interactions with clients. Your brand personality is the set of human characteristics and emotions associated with your practice. Clearly defining your values and personality helps you create a brand that feels authentic, relatable, and attractive to your ideal clients.

To identify your brand values, ask yourself,

- *What beliefs and principles are nonnegotiable in my practice?*
- *What do I stand for as a therapist and as a person?*
- *What values do I want my practice to embody and promote?*

To define your brand personality, consider,
- *If my practice were a person, what adjectives would I use to describe them?*
- *What emotions do I want my clients to feel when interacting with my brand?*
- *How do I want to be perceived by my target audience?*

Ensuring Consistency. Once you've defined the key elements of your brand identity, ensuring consistency across all your marketing channels is essential. Consistency breeds familiarity and trust, making it easier for potential clients to recognize and remember your practice.

To maintain brand consistency, be sure to do the following:

- **Develop brand guidelines.** Create a document outlining your visual identity, voice, messaging, values, and personality.
- **Create templates and assets.** Develop branded templates and assets for consistent use across all channels.
- **Regularly audit your branding.** Periodically review your marketing materials, website, and social media presence to ensure they reflect your brand identity. Make adjustments as needed.

Remember, building a strong brand identity is an ongoing process. As your practice grows and evolves, so should your branding. Stay attuned to your audience's needs and preferences, and adapt your brand identity accordingly.

By investing time and effort to develop a strong, authentic brand identity, you lay the foundation for all your marketing efforts. A well-defined brand attracts the right clients, builds trust and credibility, and sets your practice apart in a crowded market. In the following sections, we'll explore how to apply your brand identity to your website and other marketing channels to create a cohesive, client-attracting presence.

MAKING YOUR WEBSITE THE HEART OF YOUR ONLINE PRESENCE

No matter where you're engaging with potential clients— whether through social media, local directories, or networking events—all roads lead back to your website. Your website is the central hub of your online presence. It is the primary destination for potential clients to learn more about your practice and the transformative experience they can expect when working with you.

Think of your website as the online embodiment of your practice. It's where potential clients go to get a sense of who you are, what you offer, and how you can help them overcome their challenges and achieve their goals. More than just a digital brochure, your website tells a story of the transformative journey your clients can expect when they work with you.

That's why it's crucial to create a client-centered website that resonates with your ideal clients and paints a compelling picture of the transformation they seek. Every element of your website, from the design and messaging to the user experience and calls to action, should be crafted with your ideal client in mind.

Tailoring Your Website to Your Ideal Client

In the previous chapter, you developed a deep understanding of your ideal client—their needs, challenges, and aspirations. Now, it's time to use this knowledge to inform every aspect of your website, from the design and layout to the content and messaging.

Consider the following ways to tailor your website to your ideal client:

- Use language and a tone that resonates with your target audience. If your ideal clients are corporate professionals seeking stress management techniques, use language that speaks to their specific challenges and goals.
- Highlight the services and specialties that are most relevant to your ideal client. For example, if you specialize in couples therapy, make sure this is prominently featured on your website.
- Use visuals that appeal to your target audience. If your ideal clients are creative professionals, consider incorporating artistic, visually striking elements into your website design.
- Create content that addresses your ideal client's most pressing questions and concerns. If your target audience is new parents, develop blog posts or resources that offer guidance on common parenting challenges.

By infusing every element of your website with your understanding of your ideal client, you'll create an online presence that feels tailor-made for the people you're most excited to serve.

Crafting Clear and Compelling Messaging

With a deep understanding of your ideal client in mind, it's time to develop clear, compelling messaging that communicates your unique value proposition. Your messaging should be woven throughout your website, from the headline on your home page to your service descriptions and blog posts.

To create compelling messaging, focus on the benefits and transformations your clients can expect from working with you. Use language that is warm, empathetic, and easy to understand. Avoid jargon or clinical terms that may be confusing or off-putting to potential clients.

Consider the following example of compelling messaging for a therapist who specializes in helping women heal from past traumas:

Reclaim Your Strength, Rewrite Your Story

"As a therapist with over a decade of experience, I'm here to help you navigate the painful experiences of your past and create a brighter, more empowered future. Through our work together, you'll develop the tools and insights you need to heal, grow, and thrive. You don't have to carry the weight of your trauma alone—let's work together to help you reclaim your strength and rewrite your story."

This messaging is effective because it

- speaks directly to the target audience (women who have experienced trauma)
- emphasizes the transformative benefits of therapy (healing, empowerment, growth)
- uses language that is warm, supportive, and easy to understand

- offers a clear call to action (inviting the reader to work with the therapist to achieve their goals)

As you develop your messaging, keep your ideal client in mind. What do they need to hear? What will resonate with their experiences and motivate them to take action?

Designing a User-Friendly Experience

In addition to compelling messaging, your website's design and navigation play a crucial role in engaging and retaining potential clients. A user-friendly website is one that is easy to navigate, is visually appealing, and provides a seamless experience across all devices.

When designing your website, prioritize simplicity and clarity. Use a clean, uncluttered layout with plenty of white space to guide the user's eye toward key information. Organize your content logically and intuitively, with clear headings and subheadings to break up text and make it easy to scan.

Incorporate visuals strategically throughout your site to create an inviting, engaging experience. Use high-quality images and videos that reflect your brand personality and help potential clients connect with you on a personal level. For example, you might include high-quality photos of your office space to give visitors a sense of the warm, welcoming environment they can expect when working with you.

Ensure that your website is optimized for mobile devices, as more and more people are accessing the internet on their smartphones and tablets. A responsive design that adapts to different screen sizes will provide a seamless experience for all users, regardless of how they access your site.

Finally, make it easy for potential clients to contact you. Include clear calls to action throughout your site, such as "Schedule a Consultation" or "Learn More About Our

Services." Provide multiple ways to get in touch, such as a contact form, phone number, and email address.

By prioritizing user-friendliness in your website design, you'll create a welcoming, engaging experience that encourages potential clients to explore your site and take the next step in working with you.

Creating Valuable, Relevant Content

In addition to your core website pages like your home page, about page, and service descriptions, it's important to regularly create valuable, relevant content that showcases your expertise and provides helpful resources for your target audience. This can include blog posts, articles, infographics, videos, and more.

By consistently publishing high-quality content, you'll establish yourself as a trusted authority in your field, build relationships with potential clients, and improve your website's search engine rankings. When developing your content strategy, consider the following best practices:

1. Identify key topics and questions that are relevant to your ideal clients. What challenges are they facing? What information are they seeking? Use these insights to guide your content creation.
2. Develop a consistent posting schedule to keep your website fresh and engaging. Aim to publish new content at least once a week, whether it's a blog post, video, or other resource.
3. Optimize your content for search engines by incorporating relevant keywords and using clear headings and subheadings.

- Promote your content across your social media channels to drive traffic back to your website and engage your audience.

Here's an example of how you might put these content strategies into action.

Let's say you're a therapist who specializes in helping adults manage anxiety. You might create a series of blog posts on topics like these:

- "5 Simple Mindfulness Techniques to Calm Anxiety"
- "The Link Between Diet and Anxiety: What You Need to Know"
- "How to Support a Loved One Struggling with Anxiety"

Each post would provide valuable, actionable tips and insights for your target audience while also incorporating relevant keywords like "anxiety management," "mindfulness techniques," and "support for anxiety."

By consistently creating valuable content, you'll attract more of your ideal clients to your website, establish your expertise, and build trust and credibility with your audience.

Crafting a Website That Resonates and Converts

Creating a client-attracting website is an ongoing process that requires regular attention and refinement. By leveraging your understanding of your ideal client, crafting compelling messaging, designing a user-friendly experience, and creating valuable content, you'll build a powerful online presence that resonates with your target audience and positions you as the go-to therapist in your niche.

Remember, your website is often the first impression potential clients have of your practice. By investing time and effort in creating a website that truly reflects your unique value and expertise, you'll attract more of your ideal clients and build a thriving, fulfilling practice.

In the next section, we'll explore how search engine optimization (SEO) can enhance your website's visibility and performance, helping you reach more of your ideal clients through organic search traffic.

OPTIMIZING YOUR WEBSITE FOR SEARCH ENGINES (SEO)

You've poured your heart and soul into creating a website that perfectly represents your therapy practice. The design is welcoming, the content is engaging, and the user experience is intuitive. However, as the weeks go by, you realize that the number of inquiries from your website is lower than expected. Despite your best efforts, potential clients seem to have difficulty finding you online.

This is where search engine optimization (SEO) comes in. As the key to unlocking your website's full potential, SEO ensures that your ideal clients can easily find you when they need your services the most.

The Power of SEO for Therapists

In the world of digital marketing, SEO is a game changer. By optimizing your website for search engines like Google, you enjoy multiple benefits:

1. **Boost your online visibility.** When your website ranks higher in search results, more potential clients will discover your practice and learn about your services.

2. **Establish your credibility.** Appearing at the top of search results can help position your practice as a trusted and authoritative resource in your field.

3. **Attract your ideal clients.** By targeting specific keywords and phrases related to your niche, you can attract clients who will most likely benefit from your expertise.

4. **Gain a competitive edge.** SEO can help you stand out among other therapists and attract more clients to your practice in a crowded market.

But how exactly do you harness the power of SEO? Let's explore some key strategies.

The Building Blocks of a Strong SEO Strategy

1. **Keyword Research: The Foundation of SEO.** At the heart of any effective SEO strategy lies keyword research. This involves identifying the specific words and phrases your ideal clients use when searching for therapists online. By understanding your target audience's language, you can optimize your website to appear in their search results.

   Tools like Google Keyword Planner and SEMrush can help you uncover valuable keyword insights, such as search volume and competition level. For example, if you specialize in couples therapy, you might target keywords like "couples counseling near me" or "relationship therapy."

2. **On-Page Optimization: Weaving Keywords into Your Website.** Once you've identified your target keywords, it's time to incorporate them into your website's on-page elements strategically.

- Page titles and meta descriptions: use the keywords in your page titles and meta descriptions to help search engines understand what your pages are about. Meta titles are the clickable headlines displayed in search results, while meta descriptions provide a brief summary of the page content below the title. Together, they improve visibility and attract potential clients to click on your suite.
- Headings and subheadings: structure your content with header tags (H1, H2, H3), and include keywords in your headings and subheadings to emphasize key topics.
- Body content: incorporate your keywords naturally throughout your website's body content, aiming for a 1–2 percent keyword density. Remember, the goal is to create content that reads smoothly and provides value to your audience.

3. **Content Creation: Providing Value and Showcasing Your Expertise.** Search engines love websites that consistently publish high-quality, relevant content. By regularly creating blog posts, articles, and resources that address your ideal client's needs and showcase your expertise, you can improve your search engine rankings and attract more targeted traffic.

    As you develop your content strategy, focus on

    - addressing your ideal client's pain points and questions
    - providing actionable tips and insights related to your niche
    - incorporating your target keywords naturally throughout your content
    - using a clear, easy-to-read format with short paragraphs, bullet points, and subheadings

4. **Link Building: Establishing Your Website's Authority.** Another crucial aspect of SEO is link building. This involves acquiring links from other reputable websites that point back to your site. Search engines view these backlinks as "votes of confidence" in your website's authority and relevance.

   As you build high-quality backlinks, consider each of the following:

   - Creating valuable, shareable content that other websites will want to link to
   - Reaching out to other therapists or mental health bloggers to request a link to your content
   - Writing guest posts for other websites in your niche and including a link back to your site in your author bio
   - Participating in online communities and forums, providing helpful answers, and linking back to relevant resources on your site

5. **Local SEO: Attracting Clients in Your Area.** If you serve clients in a specific geographic location, optimizing for local SEO is essential. This involves

   - claiming and optimizing your Google Business Profile listing with your practice name, address, phone number, website, and business hours
   - including your city, state, and/or service area in your website's title tags, meta descriptions, and content
   - building local citations by listing your practice on online directories like local therapy directories

6. **Monitoring SEO: Refining Your Strategy.** SEO is an ongoing process that requires continuous monitoring and refinement. By using tools like Google Analytics and Google Search Console, you can track your

website's performance, identify areas for improvement, and make data-driven decisions to optimize your SEO strategy.

- Optimizing your website for search engines may seem daunting at first, but by breaking it down into manageable steps and consistently implementing these strategies, you can significantly improve your online visibility and attract more of your ideal clients.

- Remember, SEO is a marathon, not a sprint. It takes time, effort, and patience to see results. But by staying committed to the process and continually refining your approach, you'll gradually build a strong online presence that positions your practice as a go-to resource for the clients you're meant to serve.

LEVERAGING GOOGLE BUSINESS PROFILE FOR LOCAL VISIBILITY

While SEO is essential for improving your overall online visibility, there's another crucial tool that can significantly boost your local presence and help you attract clients in your immediate area: Google Business Profile (GBP).

Google Business Profile is a free platform provided by Google that allows businesses, including therapy practices, to manage their online presence across Google's various services, such as Google Search and Google Maps. By creating and optimizing your GBP listing, you can make it easier for potential clients in your local area to find, learn about, and engage with your practice.

Here are some of the benefits for therapists:

1. Increased Local Visibility—When potential clients search for therapy services in your area, a well-optimized GBP listing can help your practice appear at the top of local search results, increasing your visibility and the likelihood of attracting new clients.

2. Enhanced Online Reputation—GBP allows clients to leave reviews of your practice, which can help build trust and credibility with potential clients. Positive reviews can serve as powerful social proof, encouraging others to choose your practice over competitors.

3. Valuable Insights—GBP provides valuable analytics and insights about how clients are interacting with your profile, such as how they found your listing and what actions they took (e.g., visiting your website, calling your practice). These insights can help you refine your online marketing strategies and make data-driven decisions.

4. Improved Client Engagement—GBP enables you to share updates, special offers, and valuable content directly with your local audience, helping you stay top of mind and build relationships with potential and existing clients.

To optimize the benefits of Google Business Profile, it's essential to create a complete, accurate, and compelling profile that showcases your practice in the best possible light. Here are some key steps to optimize your profile:

1. **Claim and verify your listing.** If you haven't already, claim your practice's GBP listing and verify your ownership by going to https://www.google.com/business/.

2. **Complete your profile.** Fill out all relevant information about your practice, including your practice name, address, phone number, website URL, hours of operation, and a detailed description of your services. The more complete and accurate your profile, the more likely it is to appear in relevant local searches.

3. **Choose the right categories.** Select the most relevant categories for your practice, such as "Psychologist," "Marriage Counselor," or "Mental Health Service." Choosing the right categories helps Google understand what your practice offers and display it in the most relevant search results.

4. **Add photos and videos**. Enhance your profile with high-quality photos and videos of your practice, such as images of your office space, team members, or therapeutic activities. Visual content can help potential clients get a sense of your practice's atmosphere and personality, making them more likely to engage with your profile.

5. **Share regular updates.** Use GBP's posting feature to share updates, blog posts, special offers, or announcements with your local audience. Regular activity on your profile can help keep your practice top of mind and encourage potential clients to take action.

6. **Monitor your insights.** Regularly review your GBP insights to understand how clients are finding and interacting with your profile. Use this data to inform your online marketing strategies and continuously improve your profile's performance.

Integrating Google Business Profile with Your Overall Online Presence

While Google Business Profile is a powerful tool on its own, it's most effective when integrated with your other online marketing efforts, such as your website and social media profiles. Here are some ways to ensure a cohesive online presence:

1. Consistency—Ensure that your practice's name, address, phone number, and other key information are consistent across your GBP listing, website, and other online directories. Inconsistent information can confuse potential clients and harm your local search rankings.
2. Cross-promotion—Include a link to your GBP listing on your website and encourage website visitors to check out your Google reviews. Similarly, use your GBP posts to drive traffic back to your website by sharing blog posts, special offers, or other valuable content.
3. Integration with other Google services—Optimize your practice's presence across other Google services, such as Google Maps and Google Search. For example, ensure that your practice appears on Google Maps with accurate information and directions, and consider using Google Ads to further boost your visibility in local search results.

By leveraging Google Business Profile and integrating it with your overall online presence, you can significantly improve your practice's local visibility, attract more potential clients in your area, and build a strong, trustworthy online reputation.

REFLECT AND TAKE ACTION

Congratulations on completing this chapter on effective marketing strategies to attract your ideal clients! The insights and strategies you've gained throughout this chapter will serve as a solid foundation for building a strong online presence and connecting with the clients you're most passionate about serving.

Key Takeaways
- Developing a strong brand identity is the first step in creating a cohesive and memorable presence that resonates with your ideal clients and distinguishes you from other therapists in your niche.
- Your website is the cornerstone of your online marketing efforts. It serves as the primary destination for potential clients to learn about your services and the transformative experience they can expect when working with you.
- Search engine optimization (SEO) is a crucial aspect of online marketing that helps potential clients find your website when searching for the services you offer.
- Leveraging Google Business Profile can significantly enhance your local online presence, making it easier for potential clients in your area to discover and connect with your practice.

Action Steps
1. **Define your brand identity.** Before diving into creating your website or other marketing materials, take time to clarify your brand identity. Reflect on your values, your unique approach to therapy, and the qualities that set you apart from other therapists. Use these

insights to inform your visual identity, messaging, and overall online presence.

2. **Create a client-focused website.** As you develop your website, keep your ideal client at the forefront of your mind. Craft content that speaks directly to their needs, challenges, and aspirations, and use storytelling to paint a vivid picture of the transformative experience they can expect when working with you. Prioritize user-friendly design and clear calls to action to guide potential clients through your site.

3. **Implement basic SEO practices.** While SEO can seem daunting at first, start by focusing on the basics. Conduct keyword research to identify the terms your ideal clients use when searching for therapy services, and incorporate these keywords naturally throughout your website's content, titles, and headers. Ensure your website is mobile friendly and loads quickly to provide a positive user experience.

4. **Claim your Google Business Profile listing.** Set up your Google Business Profile listing, complete with accurate information about your practice, high-quality photos, and a compelling description of your services. Regularly post updates to keep your listing active and engaging.

5. **Commit to ongoing learning and refinement.** Building a strong online presence is an ongoing process that requires continuous learning and adaptation. As you implement these marketing strategies, stay open to feedback, track your progress, and be willing to adjust your approach based on insights and results.

Remember, attracting your ideal clients through effective marketing is a journey, not a destination. By consistently applying the principles and strategies outlined in this chapter, you'll gradually build a powerful online presence that resonates with your target audience and positions you for long-term success in private practice.

Creating a strong online presence is just one aspect of building a thriving practice. In the next chapter, we'll explore additional strategies for expanding your reach and impact through networking, social media marketing, online directories, and community engagement. By combining your newly acquired online marketing knowledge with proactive outreach and relationship building, you'll create a powerful foundation for a successful and sustainable private practice.

Get ready to go deeper into the world of marketing and networking as we uncover even more opportunities to connect with your ideal clients and make a lasting difference in their lives.

8

MARKETING STRATEGIES TO EXPAND YOUR REACH

The previous chapter explored the importance of creating a strong online presence through your website, SEO, and your Google Business Profile listing. These strategies form the foundation of your marketing efforts, helping potential clients find and connect with your practice.

Now it's time to take your marketing to the next level by leveraging the power of networking, social media, and online directories.

While having a well-optimized website is crucial, it's only one piece of the puzzle. You must actively engage with your target audience across multiple channels to expand your reach and attract your ideal clients. Combining your online presence with strategic networking, social media marketing, and directory listings will create a powerful, interconnected web of opportunities to showcase your expertise.

These are strategies you will want to explore and implement:

1. Networking—building authentic relationships within your professional community to expand your referral network and establish your practice as a trusted resource

2. Social Media—leveraging platforms like Facebook and Instagram to connect with your ideal clients, share valuable content, and build a loyal following
3. Online Directories—maximize your visibility on therapy-specific directories to attract clients actively seeking mental health support

By implementing these strategies alongside your website and SEO efforts, you'll create a comprehensive, multifaceted marketing approach that positions your practice for sustainable growth and success.

Let's take a look at all three.

THE ART OF NETWORKING FOR THERAPISTS

As a therapist starting a private practice, networking is essential to building professional relationships, expanding your referral network, and establishing your practice as a trusted resource within the mental health community.

By cultivating a strong network, you can expand your knowledge and expertise through shared insights and experiences. A well-developed network increases your visibility and credibility within the mental health community, helping to establish your reputation as a trusted provider. It also allows you to build a robust referral network to support your practice's growth, and creates opportunities for collaboration and professional development, enhancing both your skills and the services you offer.

Networking is more than just exchanging business cards and attending events. It's about building genuine, mutually beneficial relationships with other professionals who share your values and commitment to helping others. Effective networking is rooted in authentic, mutually beneficial relationships. To build strong connections with colleagues and referral sources, do these things:

- Approach networking with a mindset of curiosity, openness, and generosity.
- Focus on learning about others' experiences, challenges, and goals, and look for ways to provide support or resources.
- Share your insights, successes, and struggles openly and honestly.
- Follow up after events or meetings to express your appreciation and continue the conversation.
- Maintain relationships by staying in touch regularly, sharing relevant articles or resources, and expressing interest in your colleagues' work.

Remember, networking is an ongoing process that requires consistent effort and a genuine commitment to supporting others' growth and success. Making networking a priority and approaching it with an open, generous mindset will create a strong foundation for your practice's long-term success.

So, where can you find networking opportunities where you can build these authentic relationships? Below are three places to start.

1. *Online Networking*

In today's digital age, online networking has become essential for connecting with colleagues and referral sources. Here are some ways to make the most of online networking opportunities:

- Join professional online communities such as LinkedIn or Facebook groups related to your specialty or focused on running a private practice.
- Participate in discussions by sharing your insights, experiences, and resources.
- Attend virtual conferences and webinars to learn from experts and connect with colleagues from around the world.
- Engage with colleagues' content by commenting on their posts, sharing their articles, and providing thoughtful feedback.

One valuable resource for online networking is the "Solo Practice Success" Facebook group, which I created to provide a supportive community for therapists in private practice. This group offers opportunities to connect with colleagues, share resources, and participate in a community directory to increase your visibility and referral network.

2. *Local Events and Organizations*

While online networking is valuable, in-person connections are essential for building lasting relationships. Here are some ways to make the most of local networking opportunities:

- Attend workshops, conferences, and seminars hosted by local therapy organizations or universities.
- Join local chapters of national therapy organizations, such as the American Association for Marriage and Family Therapy (AAMFT) or the National Association of Social Workers (NASW).
- Participate in peer consultation groups or case study discussions to learn from colleagues and build relationships.

- Volunteer for leadership roles or committees within local organizations to demonstrate your commitment to the field and expand your network.

When attending events or participating in organizations, focus on building genuine connections rather than simply collecting business cards. Take the time to learn about your colleagues' specialties, experiences, and goals, and look for ways to support one another's growth and success.

3. *Community Outreach to Deepen Your Local Impact*

As a therapist starting a private practice, your impact extends beyond the walls of your office. By engaging in community outreach, you can connect with individuals and organizations that need your expertise, increase your visibility, and make a meaningful difference in your local community.

Community outreach involves sharing your knowledge, skills, and resources with the broader public through various activities and initiatives. By participating in outreach efforts, you can

- increase awareness about mental health and the benefits of therapy,
- reduce stigma and barriers to seeking help,
- establish your practice as a trusted resource within the community,
- build relationships with potential clients, referral sources, and community partners, and
- make a positive impact on the lives of individuals and families in your area.

One way to engage with your community is by *participating in local events*, such as health fairs, school functions, or community festivals. Here are some tips for making the most of these opportunities:

- Research upcoming events that align with your practice's mission and target audience.
- Contact event organizers to inquire about opportunities to participate, such as hosting a booth or giving a presentation.
- Prepare engaging, informative materials to share with attendees, such as brochures, handouts, or giveaways.
- Focus on providing value and building relationships rather than simply promoting your services.
- Follow up with individuals who express interest in learning more about your practice.

Another effective outreach strategy is ***hosting educational workshops or seminars*** on mental health and well-being. Here are some steps for planning and executing successful workshops:

- Identify issues that align with your expertise and the needs of your community.
- Partner with local organizations, such as schools, libraries, or community centers, to host the event.
- Promote the workshop through social media, email, and community bulletin boards.
- Prepare engaging, interactive content that provides practical tips and resources.
- Encourage attendees to ask questions and share their own experiences.
- Provide information about your practice and how to access your services.

A third way to impact your community is by **contributing expert commentary**. As a mental health professional, you have valuable insights and perspectives to share with your community. Here are some ways to contribute your expertise through local media and publications:

- Reach out to local journalists or editors to offer your commentary on mental health topics.
- Write op-eds or articles for local newspapers or magazines.
- Participate in interviews or news segments related to your areas of expertise.
- Share your media appearances and publications on your website and social media channels.
- Position yourself as a go-to resource for mental health information and guidance.

You can also engage in community outreach by **collaborating with organizations**. Partnering with local organizations can help you expand your reach and impact while building valuable relationships within your community. Here are some types of organizations to consider collaborating with:

- Schools and universities
- Health care providers and hospitals
- Nonprofit organizations focused on mental health or related issues
- Employee assistance programs and workplace wellness initiatives
- Faith-based organizations

When approaching potential partners, focus on finding ways to support their mission and provide value to their constituents. For example, offer to conduct a staff training, lead support groups, or develop educational resources.

Let me also say this.

When engaging with your local community, if you want to build trust and credibility, it's imperative to show consistency in your commitment. What does this look like in practical terms?

- Participating on a regular basis
- Following through on commitments and promises
- Communicating clearly and promptly with partners and collaborators
- Seeking feedback and adapting your approach as needed
- Celebrating successes and milestones with your community

You'll establish your practice as a valued and trusted resource within your community by showing up consistently and demonstrating your dedication to making a positive impact.

Effective community outreach also requires a willingness to listen and adapt to your community's changing needs and priorities. To stay responsive and relevant, consider taking these actions:

- Regularly soliciting feedback from partners, collaborators, and community members
- Staying informed about local issues, challenges, and opportunities
- Adapting your outreach strategies and messages to reflect current needs and concerns

- Being open to new ideas and approaches that align with your mission and values
- Continuously evaluating and refining your outreach efforts based on results and feedback

By listening closely to your community and adapting your approach as needed, you'll ensure that your outreach efforts remain effective, meaningful, and impactful over time.

Effective community outreach requires a commitment to building relationships, providing value, and making a positive impact over time. By approaching outreach with authenticity, consistency, and a willingness to listen and adapt, therapists can deepen their local impact and build a strong foundation for long-term success and fulfillment in their work.

In the next section, we'll explore how social media marketing can help therapists expand their reach further, connecting with potential clients and referral sources beyond their local community.

LEVERAGING SOCIAL MEDIA TO BUILD YOUR BRAND AND ESTABLISH EXPERTISE

Social media offers an unparalleled opportunity for therapists starting a private practice to build their brand, establish credibility, and connect with potential clients. Unlike traditional marketing methods, social media allows for direct, real-time interaction with your audience. Here are some key benefits of using social media as a marketing tool:

- Broader Reach—Social media platforms have vast user bases, allowing you to reach a wider audience than you could through in-person networking or traditional advertising.

- Cost-Effective—Setting up and maintaining social media profiles is generally free or low-cost compared to other forms of marketing, making it an accessible option for new practices.
- Engagement and Interaction—Social media allows you to interact with your audience in real time, answering questions and building relationships that can lead to client referrals.
- Credibility Building—Regularly sharing valuable content and insights can position you as an expert, increasing trust and credibility among potential clients.

Catering Content to Your Ideal Client

To maximize the effectiveness of your social media efforts, it's crucial to tailor your content to your ideal client. Here's how to do that:

- **Understand their needs.** Identify your ideal client's specific issues and challenges. This could include anxiety management, relationship issues, or stress reduction. By understanding their needs, you can create content that addresses their pain points.
- **Speak their language.** Use language and terminology that resonates with your ideal clients. Avoid confusing jargon, and instead, use clear and relatable language that makes your content accessible.
- **Highlight solutions.** Focus on how your services can help solve their problems. Share tips, advice, and insights that provide real value and demonstrate your expertise in addressing their concerns.

Choosing the Right Platforms

Selecting the appropriate social media platforms ensures your content reaches your ideal client. Each platform has its strengths and caters to different demographics:

- Instagram—Great for visually engaging content and reaching a younger audience. Use it to share inspirational quotes, tips, and short videos that highlight your practice's personality and approach.
- Facebook—Ideal for community engagement and sharing longer posts. It's also helpful in discussing mental health topics in depth, hosting Q&A sessions, and promoting events.
- LinkedIn—Best for professional networking and connecting with other mental health professionals. Share articles and industry insights, and engage in professional groups.
- X—Useful for sharing quick tips and updates and engaging in discussions on mental health topics. It's also a good platform for staying updated on industry news and trends.

Creating Valuable Content

Creating content that provides value to your ideal client is key to building trust and showcasing your expertise. Here are some strategies:

- Educational Posts—Share information on common mental health issues, therapeutic techniques, and wellness tips. This helps potential clients see you as a knowledgeable and reliable resource.

- Regular Updates—Post regularly to maintain an active presence. This keeps your audience engaged and ensures that your practice stays top of mind.
- Varied Content Types—Use a mix of text posts, images, videos, and infographics to keep your content interesting and accessible. Different types of content can help convey complex information more effectively.

Ensuring Clarity and Compliance

When using social media as a therapist, it's essential to distinguish clearly between providing information and offering therapy. Follow these guidelines to maintain ethical and professional boundaries:

- **Include disclaimers**. Clearly state that the information provided on your social media is for educational purposes only and does not constitute professional therapy. Include a disclaimer on all your profiles and posts.
- **State licensing information.** Indicate which states you are licensed to practice in. This helps avoid confusion and ensures that potential clients understand where you can legally provide services.
- **Identify your ideal client.** Make it clear who you serve. Whether it's individuals struggling with anxiety, couples seeking relationship counseling, or families in need of support, stating this explicitly helps attract the right clients.
- **Communicate your approach.** Explain your therapeutic approach and philosophy. This helps potential clients understand how you work and whether your approach aligns with their needs.

- **Provide clear calls to action.** Encourage potential clients to take the next step. This could be scheduling a consultation, visiting your website for more information, or contacting you directly for inquiries.
- **Provide link to your website.** Ensure that all your social media profiles include a link to your website where potential clients can find more detailed information about your services and how to book an appointment.

Setting Yourself Up for Success

To leverage social media effectively, ensure that you are set up for success with a strategic approach:

- **Create professional profiles.** Set up profiles that reflect your brand and professional identity. Use consistent branding across all platforms, including your photo, bio, and contact information.
- **Use analytics.** Review your posts' performance regularly to understand what content resonates most with your audience. Use these insights to refine your content strategy and improve engagement.
- **Engage with followers.** Actively engage with your audience by responding to comments, answering questions, and participating in discussions. Building relationships through engagement helps establish trust and can lead to more referrals and client inquiries.

Leveraging social media effectively can help you build your brand, establish your authority, and connect with your ideal clients. By creating valuable content, selecting the right platforms, and maintaining ethical clarity, you can use social media to grow your practice and enhance your professional reputation. Embrace the strategies above to maximize your reach and impact, ensuring your expertise is accessible to those who need it most.

MAXIMIZING YOUR IMPACT WITH ONLINE DIRECTORY PROFILES

Online directories serve as a primary resource for potential clients seeking therapy. As someone who has launched a provider directory and booking platform, Ravel Mental Health, I can attest to the importance of these directories in making it easier for people to find a mental health provider and schedule an appointment. This mission is near and dear to my heart. I firmly believe that having a well-crafted profile increases your visibility and provides an opportunity to connect genuinely with your ideal clients, guiding them toward taking the first step in their therapeutic journey with you.

However, many profiles miss the mark due to common pitfalls:

1. Therapist-centered content—Focusing too much on the therapist's credentials and achievements without addressing the client's needs and struggles.
2. Lack of client focus—Failing to center the profile on what the client is experiencing.
3. Too broad—Trying to appeal to everyone can result in speaking to no one.
4. Weak call to action—Without a clear, compelling invitation to take the next step, potential clients may leave your profile without making contact.

I have developed the Client Connection Framework, a step-by-step approach I teach to the therapists I coach, to help them create profiles that effectively connect with and convert potential clients. This valuable tool will ensure your profile is focused and client centered and speaks directly to the needs and aspirations of your ideal clients. It is built around three key sections designed to work together to create a compelling and engaging profile:

1. Your Ideal Client—Begin by articulating your ideal client's specific challenges and goals. Demonstrate a deep understanding of who you serve by highlighting the main issues, symptoms, and motivations that bring them to seek therapy. Address any hesitations or fears they may have about starting the process, showing that you understand their concerns.

2. How You Can Help—Next, showcase your therapeutic approach, philosophy, and specific techniques. Clearly explain how you work and the outcomes you facilitate, establishing your credibility and illustrating the transformative journey you offer. Emphasize how you collaborate with clients to help them achieve their goals and create a safe, judgment-free environment for them to explore their challenges. This section should give potential clients a clear picture of what they can expect when working with you.

3. Reach Out—Finally, craft a compelling call to action that invites potential clients to take the next step. Make this step irresistible and easy to take, whether it's scheduling a consultation or simply reaching out for more information. Communicate your understanding of clients' vulnerabilities around seeking help. This section should encourage potential clients to take action and begin their journey toward better mental health.

By following the Client Connection Framework, you can create a profile that resonates with your ideal clients, addresses their concerns, and encourages them to take the first step in seeking help. This framework ensures that your profile is not only informative but also engaging and compelling, increasing the likelihood of converting potential clients into actual clients.

In addition to the Client Connection Framework, optimize your directory profile by including these key elements:

- Professional Headshot—Include a high-quality, welcoming photo that conveys confidence and relatability.
- Certifications—List all relevant certifications to enhance your credibility and expertise.
- Introductory Video—Add a short professional video to distinguish your profile and establish a quicker connection with potential clients.
- Complete Contact Information—Ensure your profile includes comprehensive, up-to-date contact information, making it easy for potential clients to reach you. Be sure there is a link to your website so they can learn more about you and your practice and schedule an appointment.
- Consistent Online Presence—Regularly update your profile and ensure it aligns with your other online representations to maintain a professional image and a consistent message.

By thoughtfully crafting your directory profile using the Client Connection Framework and incorporating these key elements, you will create a magnetic online presence that resonates with your ideal clients and guides them toward choosing you as their therapist.

MEASURING AND REFINING YOUR MARKETING EFFORTS

After expanding your reach through networking, social media, and online directories, it's crucial to measure the impact of these activities and refine your strategies accordingly. This process helps you understand what's working, what isn't, and how you can improve your efforts to connect more effectively with potential clients.

Using Metrics to Understand the Impact

For therapists starting out, it's vital to monitor the effectiveness of your marketing efforts without overwhelming yourself with complex analytics. Focus on simple, meaningful metrics that provide insights into your marketing activities:

- Engagement on social media—Track likes, comments, and shares to see what types of content resonate with your audience.
- Referrals from networking—Note which networking activities (online groups, local events) lead to new client inquiries or collaborations.
- Directory Traffic—Some online directories provide metrics on how many people viewed your profile, clicked on your contact information, or directly contacted you.

Keeping your technology comfort level and budget in mind, here are some tools you can use to track and measure the traction you are getting:

- Google analytics—A basic setup can help you track visits to your website and understand how users find you.
- Social media insights—Platforms like Facebook and LinkedIn offer built-in tools to track engagement and audience growth.
- Feedback and inquiry tracking—Keep a simple spreadsheet to log where inquiries and new clients are coming from, whether from social media, directories, or networking events.

Analyzing Feedback and Making Adjustments

Regularly take time to review the data and feedback you've collected:

- Monthly check-ins—Spend an hour each month reviewing your engagement metrics and inquiry sources. Look for trends, such as an increase in inquiries after a particular networking event or a well-received social media post.
- Client feedback—During initial consultations, ask clients how they found you. This direct feedback can be invaluable.
- Refine and experiment—If certain strategies are clearly working, consider putting more effort into them. Conversely, don't be afraid to scale back or tweak those that aren't bringing results.

Keeping It Manageable

As a new private practice, you should focus on building relationships and establishing a reputation, not getting bogged down by complex metrics. Keep your measurement and refinement process simple and manageable:

- **Focus on key metrics.** Instead of tracking everything, choose two or three key indicators of success that are most relevant to your goals.
- **Set realistic goals.** Set achievable marketing goals based on your capacity and the scale of your practice. This could be as simple as gaining ten new followers a month on social media or attending one networking event per quarter.
- **Ask for peer input.** Sometimes, getting an outside perspective can help. Discuss your marketing strategies with fellow therapists or a mentor to get feedback and new ideas.

For therapists launching a private practice, effective marketing is about finding what works best for you and your potential clients. By regularly measuring and refining your efforts, you can ensure that your marketing activities are both manageable and impactful, helping you build a strong foundation for your practice.

REFLECT AND TAKE ACTION

In this chapter, we've explored the importance of expanding your reach and growing your practice through networking, social media marketing, and online directories. These strategies, when combined with your foundational efforts in website development, SEO, and local search optimization, create a comprehensive marketing approach that helps you connect with your ideal clients and build a thriving practice.

Throughout our discussion, we've emphasized the significance of building authentic relationships, showcasing your expertise, and maximizing your visibility to attract more of your ideal clients. We've also highlighted the need for patience, persistence, and a commitment to continuous learning and refinement as you navigate the journey of growing your practice through effective marketing.

Key Takeaways
- Networking is about building meaningful relationships that support your professional growth, expand your referral network, and contribute to the mental health community.
- Social media marketing allows you to showcase your expertise, build trust with potential clients, and attract more of your ideal clients to your practice.
- Online therapy directories provide targeted exposure to individuals actively seeking mental health support, increasing your visibility and credibility.
- Consistently monitoring, measuring, and refining your marketing efforts is crucial for making data-driven decisions and improving your ROI (return on investment).

Action Steps
1. Expand your professional network:
   - Join relevant online communities, such as therapy-focused Facebook or LinkedIn groups, and actively participate in discussions.
   - Attend at least one local networking event per quarter, such as workshops, conferences, or seminars hosted by professional organizations in your field.
   - Identify potential referral partners in complementary fields, such as primary care physicians or school counselors, and reach out to introduce yourself and your services.

2. Enhance your social media presence:
   - Choose at least one social media platform that aligns with your target audience and goals, such as Facebook, Instagram, or LinkedIn.
   - Develop a content calendar for the next month, focusing on providing valuable, engaging content that addresses your ideal client's needs and showcases your expertise.
   - Set aside dedicated time to engage with your followers, respond to comments and messages, and monitor your analytics to refine your strategy.
3. Optimize your online directory profiles:
   - Research and select reputable online therapy directories that cater to your niche and target audience.
   - Create or update your profiles on these directories using the Client Connection Framework, crafting compelling descriptions that speak directly to your ideal client's needs and motivations.
   - Regularly review and refine your directory profiles to ensure they remain up-to-date, professional, and effective in attracting your ideal clients.
4. Implement a measurement and refinement process:
   - Identify the key metrics you want to track for each marketing channel, such as referrals received, social media engagement, or directory profile views.
   - Set up simple tracking tools, like a spreadsheet for referrals or Google Analytics for website traffic, to monitor your progress and gather insights.
   - Schedule a monthly review of your marketing data to assess what's working, what's not, and where you can make improvements to optimize your efforts.

5. Stay committed to ongoing learning and growth:
   - Regularly seek out opportunities to expand your knowledge and skills in marketing, such as attending workshops, reading industry blogs, or taking online courses.
   - Stay open to experimenting with new strategies and tactics, and be willing to adapt your approach based on your results and insights.
   - Seek feedback and support from colleagues, mentors, and professional communities to help you navigate challenges and refine your marketing efforts.

By taking action on these steps and consistently dedicating time and effort to your marketing strategies, you'll be well on your way to expanding your reach, attracting more of your ideal clients, and building a thriving, impactful practice.

Remember, growing your practice through effective marketing is a journey, not a destination. Stay true to your unique value proposition, keep your ideal clients at the heart of every decision you make, and embrace opportunities to learn, grow, and make a meaningful difference in the lives of those you serve. With the strategies and insights you've learned in this chapter, you have the tools and knowledge you need to create a powerful, multifaceted marketing approach that sets up your practice for long-term success and sustainability.

In the next chapter, we'll explore the importance of mastering seamless practice management. As you attract more clients and grow your private practice, it's crucial to have efficient systems in place to ensure a professional, HIPAA-compliant, and client-centered experience. In the following chapter, we'll review the key aspects of effective practice management that will help you create a solid foundation for your thriving therapy practice.

9

MASTERING SEAMLESS PRACTICE MANAGEMENT

In the previous chapters, we've explored various aspects of launching and growing your private practice, from defining your niche and creating a business plan to marketing your services and building a strong online presence. Now it's time to discuss the details of practice management—the day-to-day operations that keep your business running smoothly and efficiently.

Effective practice management is the backbone of a successful therapy practice. It encompasses a wide range of tasks and responsibilities, from creating a welcoming office environment and ensuring legal compliance to streamlining your administrative processes and handling client cancellations. When done right, seamless practice management allows you to focus on what matters most, providing exceptional care to your clients and helping them achieve their goals.

In this chapter, we'll explore the key components of effective practice management and provide you with practical strategies and tools to optimize your operations. We'll discuss how to establish a welcoming physical office that promotes comfort, privacy, and accessibility for your clients and how to set up a secure virtual practice to meet the growing demand for remote services.

We'll also cover the importance of comprehensive legal compliance, including essential topics such as client forms, HIPAA guidelines, and Business Associate Agreements (BAAs). You'll learn how to select the right electronic health record (EHR) system to streamline your scheduling, clinical documentation, billing, and client communication.

To further enhance your practice's efficiency, we'll guide you through implementing digital workflows that leverage the full capabilities of your EHR system. Finally, we'll discuss best practices for preventing and handling cancellations and no-shows, helping you minimize disruptions and maintain a steady flow of clients.

By the end of this chapter, you'll have a solid understanding of the key aspects of practice management and be equipped with actionable strategies to create a thriving, client-centered practice. Let's begin exploring how you can master seamless practice management and take your practice to the next level!

ESTABLISHING A WELCOMING PHYSICAL OFFICE

For therapists who have decided to see clients in person, creating a warm, inviting, and calming environment is crucial for fostering a positive therapeutic experience. Your physical office space should reflect your professional identity and cater to the specific needs of your clientele, whether you work with adults, children, teens, couples, or groups. Here's how to make your office a sanctuary for your clients.

Choosing the Right Location
The first step in establishing your physical office is selecting a location that is convenient and accessible for your clients. Look for a space that is close to public transportation, offers ample parking, and is centrally located within the community

you serve. Additionally, ensure your office complies with the Americans with Disabilities Act (ADA) to accommodate clients with diverse needs, such as those with mobility issues or other disabilities.

Consider the surrounding environment as well. A location in a quiet neighborhood can enhance the peaceful atmosphere of your office, whereas a bustling area might add unnecessary stress for clients. Safety is another key factor; clients should feel secure coming to and leaving your office, especially during evening hours.

Designing a Therapeutic Space

When it comes to interior design, your goal is to create a space that promotes relaxation, comfort, and trust. Start by selecting furniture that is not only visually appealing but also comfortable for both you and your clients during long therapy sessions. Investing in high-quality, ergonomic seating that provides proper support can encourage a sense of safety and comfort.

- *Color and Lighting.* The colors you choose can significantly impact the mood of your space. Soft, neutral tones often promote calmness and relaxation, while brighter colors can stimulate energy and engagement. Consider using a combination of both, tailored to the specific therapeutic needs of your clientele. For instance, a play therapy room for children might feature more vibrant colors, while a space for adults might utilize soothing blues and greens.
- *Ambiance.* Lighting is another crucial element. Natural light is ideal, as it has been shown to improve mood and reduce stress. If natural light is not available, opt for soft, warm lighting rather than harsh fluorescents.

Dimmer switches can allow you to adjust the lighting to suit different times of the day and the needs of your clients.

- *Decorative Elements.* Incorporate decorative elements that reflect your therapeutic approach and resonate with your clients. Wall art, plants, and textiles can all contribute to a warm and welcoming environment. Artwork should be thoughtfully selected to evoke positive feelings or provide a point of reflection for clients. Plants not only add a touch of nature but also improve air quality and can create a sense of calm.

Practical Details

Attention to practical details can significantly enhance the functionality and comfort of your office. Consider the following:

- *Sound Management.* A high-quality sound system and soothing background music or white noise can create a calming environment and maintain privacy. Soundproofing materials, solid doors, extra wall insulation, sound-dampening materials in office décor, and white noise machines also ensure that conversations within your office cannot be overheard from outside the room.
- *Time Management.* Reliable clocks placed strategically throughout your office help you keep track of time during sessions without being obtrusive. This ensures that you maintain the therapeutic structure and manage time effectively.
- *Client Comfort.* Provide amenities such as water, tissues, and comfortable waiting areas. A well-stocked

bookshelf with a variety of reading materials can make waiting times more pleasant and less stressful.

- *Privacy and Confidentiality.* Maintaining client privacy and confidentiality is of utmost importance in any therapy practice. When designing your office layout, incorporate features that minimize the likelihood of clients encountering one another. Separate waiting areas, private entrances, or strategically placed partitions can help achieve this.
- *Trust and Credibility.* Don't underestimate the power of showcasing your qualifications and expertise in building trust and credibility with your clients. Display your licenses, certifications, and professional affiliations in a tasteful manner that aligns with your office's overall aesthetic. These should be visible but not overwhelming, reinforcing your professionalism without creating a clinical or impersonal atmosphere. You can also showcase any specialties or areas of expertise that set you apart as a therapist. This can be done subtly through the decor—such as displaying relevant books or artifacts—or in your client intake materials.

By carefully considering factors such as location, accessibility, interior design, privacy, and credibility, you can create a welcoming physical office that sets the stage for a positive and transformative therapeutic experience. Remember, the goal is to create a space where clients feel safe, valued, and understood from the moment they walk in.

In the next section, we will explore how to set up a secure virtual practice to meet the growing demand for remote therapy services.

SETTING UP A SECURE VIRTUAL PRACTICE

In today's rapidly evolving health care landscape, offering virtual therapy sessions has become increasingly important. The COVID-19 pandemic accelerated the adoption of tele-health services, making it crucial for therapists to adapt and provide remote care options to meet the needs of their clients. Virtual therapy sessions offer convenience, accessibility, and flexibility, allowing you to continue supporting your clients even when in-person meetings are not possible. However, with the benefits of virtual sessions come the responsibilities of ensuring the security, privacy, and professionalism of your remote practice.

HIPAA-Compliant Video Conferencing

When conducting virtual therapy sessions, it is essential to use a video conferencing platform that complies with the Health Insurance Portability and Accountability Act (HIPAA). HIPAA-compliant platforms, such as Zoom for Healthcare or Doxy.me, offer enhanced security features and encryption to protect sensitive client information. When selecting a platform, consider factors such as ease of use, reliability, and the availability of features like waiting rooms and screen sharing. Familiarize yourself thoroughly with the platform's settings and security options to maintain the highest level of privacy and confidentiality.

Selecting a platform that ensures secure data transmission is critical. Compliance with HIPAA means the platform has measures in place to protect patient data, such as end-to-end encryption and secure data storage. Regularly update your software to benefit from the latest security enhancements and patches. Additionally, using features like waiting rooms can control the session flow, ensuring that only the intended client is present in the virtual space.

Creating a Professional Therapeutic Setting at Home

When conducting virtual sessions from your home office, it is crucial to create a professional and therapeutic environment that closely resembles the experience of an in-person session. This requires careful consideration of your physical space, technical setup, and professional appearance.

Consider the following:

- **Designate a private space.** Choose a quiet, private room for your virtual sessions, ensuring it is free from distractions and interruptions. Inform family members or roommates about your session schedule and establish clear boundaries to maintain privacy. Using a dedicated space or room divider can help create a physical separation between your work and personal life, reinforcing professionalism.
- **Optimize your background and lighting.** The background of your virtual space should be neutral and clutter-free to avoid distractions. Consider using a plain wall, tasteful artwork, or a professional virtual background. Good lighting is essential; position yourself in front of a window to utilize natural light, or use a soft, diffused light source. Avoid harsh overhead lighting, which can cast unflattering shadows and create a less inviting atmosphere.
- **Invest in quality audio and video equipment.** Clear communication is paramount in virtual sessions. Invest in high-quality audio and video equipment to ensure your clients can see and hear you clearly. A high-resolution webcam will enhance the sense of connection,

while a headset with a noise-canceling microphone can minimize background noise and improve audio clarity. Reliable internet connectivity is also crucial to prevent interruptions during sessions.

- **Maintain professionalism in appearance and demeanor.** Your professional appearance and behavior significantly influence the therapeutic alliance in virtual settings. Dress as you would for an in-person session, ensuring your attire is appropriate and professional. Be mindful of your body language, facial expressions, and eye contact, as these nonverbal cues play a significant role in building rapport and trust with your clients in a virtual setting.

Enhancing the Virtual Therapeutic Experience

Creating a seamless virtual therapeutic experience involves more than just technical setup. It requires thoughtful engagement and a commitment to maintaining the same standards of care as in-person sessions.

Here are some things you can do that will optimize the virtual experience for your clients:

- **Engage actively with clients**. During virtual sessions, active engagement is key. Make sure to check in regularly with your clients to ensure they feel heard and understood. Use verbal affirmations and nods to show you are actively listening, and ask open-ended questions to facilitate deeper exploration of their issues.
- **Ensure privacy and confidentiality.** In addition to using a HIPAA-compliant platform, take additional measures to protect client privacy. Use strong, unique passwords for your video conferencing accounts, and change them regularly. Enable all available security

settings, such as two-factor authentication, to further safeguard your sessions.

- **Document sessions thoroughly.** Just like in-person sessions, it's essential to maintain detailed and accurate records of your virtual therapy sessions. Ensure that all documentation is stored securely and in compliance with HIPAA regulations. Consider using secure, encrypted storage solutions for digital records.
- **Provide clear instructions to clients.** Help your clients prepare for virtual sessions by providing clear instructions on how to access the video conferencing platform. Offer tips for ensuring their own privacy during the session, such as finding a quiet, private space and using headphones to prevent others from overhearing.

By setting up a secure, HIPAA-compliant virtual practice and creating a professional therapeutic environment at home, you can provide your clients with the same level of care, privacy, and confidentiality they would receive in an in-person session. Embracing virtual therapy sessions allows you to expand your reach, offer greater flexibility, and continue supporting your clients through challenging times.

In the next section, we will examine effective strategies for ensuring comprehensive legal compliance. This is essential for protecting your clients' privacy, maintaining the integrity of your practice, and minimizing the risk of legal liabilities.

ENSURING COMPREHENSIVE LEGAL COMPLIANCE

As a therapist in private practice, navigating the complex landscape of legal and ethical requirements can be challenging. However, ensuring comprehensive legal compliance is essential for protecting your clients' privacy, maintaining the integrity of your practice, and minimizing the risk of legal liabilities. This section will guide you through the key aspects of legal compliance, from developing essential client forms to understanding HIPAA guidelines and establishing Business Associate Agreements (BAAs).

Developing Essential Client Forms

A robust set of client forms is the foundation of a legally compliant practice. These essential client forms not only gather crucial information about your clients but also document their informed consent and understanding of your policies and procedures.

Intake Questionnaires: These forms collect demographic information, medical history, and treatment goals, providing a comprehensive overview of your client's needs and background. Clear, thorough intake forms can help you tailor your therapeutic approach to each client's unique circumstances.

Informed Consent Documents: These forms outline the nature of the therapeutic relationship, the limits of confidentiality, and the potential risks and benefits of treatment. Clients should sign these forms to acknowledge their understanding and agreement to participate in therapy. Informed consent is a cornerstone of ethical practice, ensuring that clients are fully aware of what to expect from their treatment. To create informed consent documents, consider starting with templates or examples available from professional organizations such as the American Psychological Association (APA) or your state's licensing board. Additionally, many therapy-specific EHR systems provide built-in templates that can be customized to reflect your practice's policies and state-specific legal requirements. If you choose to use a template, ensure it is tailored to your practice, and consult with an attorney if necessary to confirm compliance with applicable laws and ethical standards.

HIPAA Notices: These forms explain your practice's policies and procedures for protecting client privacy and confidentiality in accordance with HIPAA regulations. Clients should receive a copy of the HIPAA notice and sign an acknowledgment of receipt. This step is crucial for compliance and helps clients understand their rights regarding their health information.

Good Faith Estimate: As of January 1, 2022, the No Surprises Act requires health care providers, including therapists, to provide clients with a Good Faith Estimate (GFE) of expected charges for services. This estimate should include the expected costs of therapy sessions, assessments, and any other services that may be provided during the course of treatment. The GFE must be provided to new and continuing clients who are uninsured or self-pay, and it should be updated if there are any significant changes to the expected charges.

Release of Information Forms: These forms allow clients to authorize the sharing of their protected health information (PHI) with specific individuals or entities, such as family members, health care providers, or insurance companies.

Ensuring all these forms are properly completed and stored can help facilitate necessary communication while protecting client confidentiality. Ensure that your client forms are written in clear, concise language and are regularly reviewed and updated to reflect any changes in laws, regulations, or professional standards. Regular updates help maintain compliance and ensure that your forms meet current legal requirements.

HIPAA Guidance for PHI Handling

The Health Insurance Portability and Accountability Act (HIPAA) sets strict standards for the handling of protected health information (PHI). As a therapist, you are required to implement appropriate safeguards to ensure the confidentiality, integrity, and availability of PHI.

Secure Storage and Encryption: Implement secure storage and encryption protocols for electronic PHI, such as using password-protected devices and encrypting email communications containing sensitive information. Encryption is essential to protect data from unauthorized access during transmission and storage.

Paper Record Handling: Establish clear policies and procedures for the handling of paper records, including secure storage, access controls, and proper disposal methods (e.g., shredding). Ensure that paper records are stored in locked cabinets and only accessible to authorized personnel.

Staff Training: Train all staff members on HIPAA compliance and ensure that they understand their responsibilities for protecting client privacy. Regular training sessions can help reinforce the importance of HIPAA compliance and keep staff updated on any changes in regulations.

Breach Notification Plan: Develop a breach notification plan to address promptly any unauthorized access, use, or disclosure of PHI. This plan should outline the steps to take in the event of a breach, including notifying affected clients and relevant authorities.

Regularly review and update your HIPAA policies and procedures to ensure ongoing compliance and to address any changes in technology or regulations. Staying proactive about HIPAA compliance can help you avoid breaches and maintain client trust.

Business Associate Agreements (BAAs)

When working with third-party service providers who have access to protected health information (PHI), such as EHR platforms, billing services, or HIPAA-compliant email providers, it is crucial to execute Business Associate Agreements (BAAs). For example, a business associate could be a billing service that processes insurance claims on your behalf or an email provider that facilitates secure client communication. A BAA is a legal contract that outlines the responsibilities of the service provider (the "business associate") in protecting PHI and ensures that they adhere to the same HIPAA standards as your practice.

Review Privacy and Security Policies: Before engaging with any business associate, carefully review their privacy and security policies to ensure that they align with HIPAA requirements. This review helps ensure that the business associate has adequate safeguards in place to protect PHI.

Define Scope and Safeguards: The BAA should clearly define the scope of the business associate's access to PHI, the specific safeguards they will implement, and the steps they will take in the event of a data breach. Detailed agreements help set clear expectations and responsibilities for both parties.

Maintain and Review BAAs: Maintain a record of all BAAs, and regularly review them to ensure that they remain up-to-date and comprehensive. Periodic reviews can help you identify any necessary updates to agreements and ensure continued compliance.

By prioritizing legal compliance and implementing robust policies and procedures, you can create a safe and trusted therapeutic environment that upholds the highest standards of privacy and confidentiality. Staying informed about legal and ethical requirements and proactively addressing compliance issues will help you protect your clients, your practice, and your professional reputation.

Ensuring comprehensive legal compliance is not just about adhering to regulations; it's about fostering a professional practice built on trust, integrity, and respect for client privacy. By developing thorough client forms, adhering to HIPAA guidelines, and establishing clear BAAs, you lay a solid foundation for a legally sound and ethically robust practice. As the landscape of therapy continues to evolve, maintaining diligent compliance practices will help you navigate these changes with confidence, ensuring that your clients receive the highest standard of care.

IMPLEMENTING EFFICIENT DIGITAL WORKFLOWS

Utilizing a comprehensive, therapy-focused electronic health record (EHR) system allows you to streamline your practice management by implementing efficient digital workflows. By leveraging the full capabilities of your EHR, you can simplify processes, reduce administrative tasks, and create a seamless experience for both your clients and your practice.

Secure Client Communication and Engagement

Effective client communication is the foundation of a strong therapeutic relationship. A therapy-focused EHR should offer secure messaging, document sharing, and a client portal to facilitate seamless, HIPAA-compliant communication. Encourage your clients to use these features for communicating nonurgently, sharing resources, and accessing important information.

Set clear expectations around response times and the appropriate use of secure messaging to maintain boundaries and manage client expectations. For instance, you might inform clients that secure messages will be responded to within twenty-four hours, ensuring they understand the appropriate channels for urgent issues.

Online Booking and Appointment Management

A user-friendly online booking feature allows clients to schedule, reschedule, or cancel appointments quickly through a secure portal, reducing administrative burden on your staff. Customize your EHR's scheduling settings to reflect your practice's availability, appointment types, and durations.

Educate your clients on using the online booking feature, and encourage them to manage their appointments through the portal. Set up automated appointment reminders to reduce no-shows and last-minute cancellations. Regularly review your scheduling settings to optimize your availability and efficiency, ensuring your calendar remains balanced and manageable.

Integrated Billing and Insurance Claims Processing

Streamlining your billing and insurance claims processing is essential for maintaining a financially healthy practice. An EHR system designed for therapists should offer integrated features that automatically link client appointments, clinical notes, and billing codes, minimizing manual data entry and reducing errors. Examples of therapy-specific EHR systems you can explore include SimplePractice, TheraNest, and TherapyNotes, all of which offer billing and insurance claims features tailored to the needs of mental health professionals.

Configure your EHR's billing settings to reflect your practice's fees, billing codes, and insurance provider information. Utilize automated invoice generation, payment reminders, and insurance claims submission to save time and improve cash flow. Regularly review your financial reports within the EHR to identify any discrepancies or areas for improvement, ensuring your practice remains financially sound.

Customizable Forms and Progress Tracking

Customizable intake forms, assessments, and progress-tracking tools within your EHR can help you efficiently gather client information and monitor their progress over time. Utilize your EHR's library of pre-built forms and create custom forms tailored to your practice's unique needs.

Implement a consistent process for administering assessments and tracking client progress to inform treatment planning and measure outcomes. Regularly review and update your forms and assessments to ensure they align with best practices and evolving client needs, maintaining a high standard of care.

Reporting and Analytics

Leveraging your EHR's reporting and analytics features can provide valuable insights into your practice's performance and help you make data-driven decisions. Monitor key metrics such as appointment attendance, client engagement, and treatment outcomes to identify trends and areas for improvement.

Use financial reports to track billing and revenue, identify discrepancies, and optimize your practice's profitability. Regularly review your EHR's reporting capabilities and explore new ways to use data to inform your practice management strategies, driving continuous improvement.

Mobile Accessibility

Embrace the flexibility and convenience of mobile accessibility by utilizing your EHR's mobile app or responsive design. Access client information, update notes, and manage your schedule on the go, allowing you to work remotely and respond to client needs promptly.

Ensure that your mobile device is secure and compliant with HIPAA regulations. Establish clear boundaries around the use of mobile technology to maintain work-life balance and ensure that your practice remains professional and efficient, even when working remotely.

———

Implementing these efficient digital workflows within your therapy-focused EHR allows you to streamline your practice management, reduce administrative burdens, and dedicate more time and energy to providing exceptional client care. Continuously evaluate and refine your workflows to adapt to your practice's and clients' evolving needs. Stay informed about new features and best practices to optimize your EHR's potential, ensuring your practice remains at the forefront of digital innovation.

Now that we have discussed how to enhance practice management through digital workflows, let's explore best practices for preventing and handling cancellations and no-shows. This is a common challenge for therapists that can significantly impact client care and the financial stability of their practice.

BEST PRACTICES FOR PREVENTING AND HANDLING CANCELLATIONS AND NO-SHOWS

Cancellations and no-shows are a common challenge for private practice therapists, often leading to lost revenue, decreased productivity, and disrupted continuity of care. When clients frequently cancel or fail to attend their scheduled appointments, it can be frustrating and detrimental to both the therapeutic process and the financial stability of your practice. Implementing strategies to minimize cancellations and no-shows and having clear policies in place to handle these situations can help you maintain a thriving practice and ensure that your clients receive the consistent care they need.

Develop a Clear Cancellation Policy

Establishing a clear, written cancellation policy is crucial for setting expectations and minimizing last-minute cancellations and no-shows. Your policy should outline the minimum notice required for cancellations, typically twenty-four to forty-eight hours before the appointment, and any potential consequences for late cancellations or no-shows, such as charging a fee. It's essential to communicate your cancellation policy to clients during the intake process, have them sign an acknowledgment of understanding, and display the policy prominently in your office and on your website.

Send Appointment Reminders

Implementing an automated appointment reminder system can significantly reduce the likelihood of forgotten appointments and last-minute cancellations. Utilize your EHR's built-in reminder feature to send email and/or text reminders. Sending multiple reminders, such as a confirmation message immediately after booking, a reminder one to two days before the appointment, and a final reminder on the day of the appointment, can help ensure that clients remember and attend their scheduled sessions.

Follow Up on Missed Appointments

When a client misses an appointment, following up promptly to address any concerns and reschedule the session is essential. Reach out via phone, email, or secure messaging to express your concern for their well-being, inquire about the reason for the missed appointment, and remind them of your cancellation policy. Offer to reschedule the appointment at a mutually convenient time and discuss potential barriers to attendance, collaborating on solutions to prevent future missed appointments. By demonstrating empathy and a commitment to their care, you can strengthen the therapeutic relationship and reduce the likelihood of future no-shows.

Track and Analyze Cancellations and No-Shows

Regularly tracking and analyzing your practice's cancellation and no-show rates can help you identify patterns and potential areas for improvement. Utilize your EHR's reporting features to generate data on the overall frequency of cancellations and no-shows, the percentage of clients who consistently miss or cancel appointments, the most common reasons for cancellations or no-shows, and the effectiveness of your reminder system and cancellation policy. This data can inform targeted interventions, such as providing additional education or resources to clients who struggle with attendance, adjusting your reminder system or cancellation policy based on client feedback and behavior, and identifying and addressing any scheduling or accessibility barriers that may contribute to missed appointments.

By proactively addressing cancellations and no-shows, you can minimize disruptions to your practice, maintain a stable revenue stream, and ensure that your clients receive the consistent, high-quality care they need to achieve their therapeutic goals. Remember to approach these situations with compassion and understanding, as there may be underlying reasons for a client's inability to attend sessions consistently. Work collaboratively with your clients to find solutions that support their ongoing therapy engagement while maintaining your practice's stability and efficiency.

REFLECT AND TAKE ACTION

In this chapter, we've explored the essential components of effective practice management and provided practical strategies and tools to optimize your operations. From establishing a welcoming physical office and setting up a secure virtual practice to ensuring legal compliance, selecting the right EHR system, implementing efficient digital workflows, and handling cancellations and no-shows, mastering seamless practice management is crucial for the success and growth of your therapy practice.

Key Takeaways
- Creating a warm, inviting, and confidential physical office space promotes a positive therapeutic experience and helps clients feel comfortable and secure.
- Offering virtual therapy sessions allows you to expand your reach, provide flexibility, and continue supporting your clients, even when in-person meetings are not possible.
- Ensuring comprehensive legal compliance, including developing essential client forms, adhering to HIPAA guidelines, and executing Business Associate Agreements, protects your clients' privacy and minimizes legal risks.
- Selecting the right EHR system that prioritizes compliance, efficiency, and client-centered care streamlines your practice management and allows you to focus on providing exceptional care.
- Implementing efficient digital workflows, such as secure client communication, online booking, integrated billing, and customizable forms, reduces administrative tasks and enhances the client experience.

- Proactively addressing cancellations and no-shows through clear policies, appointment reminders, and follow-ups minimizes disruptions and ensures consistent, high-quality care for your clients.

Action Steps
1. Assess your current physical office space and identify areas for improvement regarding comfort, privacy, and accessibility. Make necessary changes to create a welcoming and therapeutic environment.
2. Research and select a HIPAA-compliant video conferencing platform for virtual therapy sessions. Set up your home office to ensure a professional and distraction-free environment.
3. Review your client forms, HIPAA policies, and Business Associate Agreements to ensure they are up-to-date and comprehensive. Make any necessary revisions and implement a system for regularly reviewing and updating these documents.
4. Evaluate your current EHR system, or research and select a new one that meets your practice's needs. Prioritize features such as compliance, customizable forms, integrated billing, and client portal access.
5. Identify areas of your practice management that can be streamlined through digital workflows. Implement features such as online booking, automated appointment reminders, and secure client messaging to enhance efficiency and client engagement.
6. Develop a clear cancellation policy and communicate it to your clients. Set up an automated appointment reminder system, and establish a protocol for following up on missed appointments.

By implementing these key takeaways and action steps, you'll be well on your way to mastering seamless practice management and creating a thriving, client-centered therapy practice. Remember, practice management is an ongoing process that requires regular evaluation and refinement. Stay informed about best practices, embrace new technologies, and continuously seek ways to optimize your operations to best serve your clients and support your professional growth.

10

BUILDING EFFECTIVE CLIENT RELATIONSHIPS FROM THE FIRST CALL

In the previous chapter, we explored the critical components of seamless practice management, from creating a welcoming office environment to implementing efficient digital workflows.

Now we'll shift our focus to one of the most crucial aspects of building a successful therapy practice: establishing strong, positive relationships with your clients from the very first interaction.

Let's begin by addressing cultural competence, determining therapist/client fit, discussing fees and insurance, setting expectations, preparing for the first session, and establishing communication and financial protocols. We'll also address how to navigate common challenges that may arise during initial client interactions.

By mastering these elements, you'll be well-equipped to create a strong foundation for effective, transformative therapeutic relationships from the first contact.

CULTURAL COMPETENCE AND ADDRESSING DIVERSE CLIENT NEEDS

As client bases become increasingly diverse, it's essential to approach each interaction with cultural humility and awareness.

Cultural competence goes beyond recognizing obvious differences; it involves a continuous process of self-reflection and openness to learning about diverse experiences and perspectives. During the consultation call and throughout the therapeutic relationship, be mindful of how cultural factors may influence a client's perception of therapy, communication style, and expectations for treatment.

Consider aspects such as language preferences, cultural beliefs about mental health, and the interaction among multiple aspects of a client's identity. For example, a client's race, ethnicity, gender, religion, and socioeconomic status may intersect uniquely, shaping his or her life experiences, challenges, and perspectives. Be aware that attitudes toward mental health and therapy can vary significantly across cultures; some clients may feel shame or stigma about seeking help, while others may have different concepts of well-being and healing. Avoid making assumptions based on any single aspect of a client's identity, and instead strive to understand how these various factors work together to inform their experiences and needs.

Be attuned to cultural differences in communication styles, family dynamics, and religious or spiritual beliefs. Throughout your interactions, practice active listening and ask respectful questions to understand better the client's cultural background and how it relates to their therapeutic needs. Be willing to acknowledge the limitations of your cultural knowledge and express a genuine interest in learning from your clients. If you feel that a client's cultural needs might be better served by another therapist, be honest and offer appropriate referrals.

Cultivating cultural competence is an ongoing process that enriches your practice and enhances your ability to provide effective, compassionate care to a diverse clientele.

THE CONSULTATION CALL

The consultation call is an essential step in building a strong therapeutic relationship. It allows both you and the client to assess fit, discuss practical details like fees and scheduling, and set clear expectations for the therapy process. This conversation lays the foundation for trust, transparency, and collaboration.

Assessing Fit

The initial consultation call is pivotal in a client's journey, setting the stage for the therapeutic process. The primary goal of the call is to determine whether there is a good fit between the therapist's expertise and approach and the client's needs and preferences. This involves actively listening to the client's concerns, asking clarifying questions, and providing a brief overview of your therapeutic style and philosophy.

During the call, focus on understanding the client's primary reasons for seeking therapy, their expectations, and any specific goals or outcomes they hope to achieve. Ask open-ended questions that encourage the client to briefly share their story and express their emotions. For example, you might ask, "What prompted you to seek therapy at this time?" or "What do you hope to gain from our work together?"

Assess the client's communication style, openness to feedback, and motivation for change. Pay attention to their tone of voice and language that may indicate hesitation or discomfort. Offer empathy and validation for their experiences and demonstrate genuine curiosity about their perspective.

Simultaneously, provide insight into your approach, highlighting your areas of specialization and the key principles guiding your work. Share a brief overview of your theoretical orientation, the techniques you typically employ, and your philosophy on the therapeutic process. Emphasize your commitment to collaboration, transparency, and tailoring the treatment plan to the client's unique needs and goals.

Be attentive to any potential red flags or indications that the client's needs may be beyond your scope of practice. Be prepared to provide appropriate referrals to other professionals or resources that may be better suited to address their specific concerns.

If, after assessing the client's needs and preferences, you determine that this is a good fit, express your enthusiasm for working together and outline the next steps in the process. If you believe another provider or approach may be more appropriate, communicate this with sensitivity and respect, emphasizing your commitment to helping the client find the best possible care.

Discussing Fees, Insurance, and Payment Options

Transparency around fees and insurance is crucial for building trust and avoiding misunderstandings. During the consultation call, offer a high-level overview of your fee structure, payment options, and any relevant insurance information. This allows the client to assess whether your services are financially feasible and aligns expectations early in the process.

Begin by briefly outlining your standard session fee, including the typical session length, whether forty-five, fifty minutes, or sixty minutes. If you provide specialized services such as couples counseling or extended sessions, mention that these have separate rates. By providing this information early on, clients clearly understand the financial commitment involved in working with you.

If you offer a sliding scale option to accommodate clients with financial constraints, note that it's available and explain that more details on eligibility can be discussed in the first session. Emphasizing your commitment to making therapy accessible while maintaining a fair fee structure can help clients feel comfortable addressing financial concerns.

For clients interested in using out-of-network insurance benefits, provide a brief explanation of how this process works. Clarify that if they choose this route, they will pay your full fee at the time of service, and you will provide a superbill. Explain that a superbill is a detailed receipt that includes necessary information required by insurance companies, such as diagnosis codes, treatment dates, and provider details, which clients can submit to their insurance company for potential reimbursement. Encourage them to contact their insurance provider about their out-of-network benefits, reimbursement rates, and any applicable deductibles.

If you are in-network with insurance providers, specify which plans you accept and confirm whether the client's plan is compatible. Let them know that specifics about copayments, deductibles, and coverage limits will be discussed in more detail in the first session after you confirm their insurance benefits.

Setting Expectations

A critical component of the consultation call is setting clear, realistic expectations for the therapeutic process. This includes discussing the frequency and duration of sessions, the anticipated length of treatment, and the level of commitment required from both therapist and client.

Explain the structure of a typical session. Describe how you typically begin sessions, such as by reviewing progress since the last meeting or discussing any current challenges or concerns. Outline your techniques or interventions, such as cognitive behavioral strategies, mindfulness practices, or expressive arts therapies.

Discuss your approach to tracking progress and adjusting the treatment plan based on the client's evolving needs and insights. Share how you monitor outcomes, such as through regular assessments, client feedback, or progress toward specific goals. Emphasize your commitment to adapting the treatment plan in collaboration with the client to ensure that therapy remains relevant, engaging, and effective.

Emphasize the importance of regular attendance and active participation in the therapeutic process. Explain how consistent engagement in therapy, both during sessions and through between-session homework or practice, is crucial for making meaningful progress and achieving desired outcomes. Discuss any potential barriers to regular attendance, such as scheduling conflicts or transportation issues, and brainstorm strategies for overcoming these challenges.

Encourage the client to ask questions and express any concerns or hesitations they may have about the therapeutic process. Create an open, nonjudgmental space for dialogue, and validate the client's feelings or apprehensions. Emphasize that therapy is a collaborative journey and that the client's input and feedback are essential for creating a tailored, effective treatment plan.

By setting clear expectations from the outset, you help the client understand their role in the therapeutic relationship and increase the likelihood of consistent engagement and positive outcomes. This transparency and open communication foster a sense of trust, safety, and shared purpose, setting the stage for a productive, transformative therapeutic experience.

FROM CONSULTATION TO NEXT STEP

As the consultation call winds down, it's important to create space for any final questions or thoughts. I often ask, "Do you have any other questions or concerns you'd like to discuss before we wrap up?" This simple question can lead to valuable insights and help ensure the potential client feels heard and understood.

Remember, while we've outlined a structured approach to these calls, it's crucial to let the conversation flow naturally. Over time, you'll find that these consultations become more fluid and intuitive. Don't worry if you don't cover every point in the exact order we've discussed—the key is to ensure that by the end of the call, both you and the potential client have the information needed to decide on the next steps.

From here, the path forward can take a few different directions.

If You Determine You're Not the Best Fit
Sometimes, despite our best intentions, we may not be the right therapist for a particular client. If this is the case, here's what you can do:

1. Explain your assessment honestly but sensitively. For example, you might say, "Based on what you've shared, I believe you might benefit more from a therapist who specializes in [specific area]."

2. Offer to provide referrals to other therapists or services that might better meet their needs.
3. Thank them for their time and openness during the consultation.

If the Client is Unsure or Decides Not to Schedule

It's common for potential clients to need time to consider their options. In this case, here's how you can respond:

1. Thank them for their time and express understanding of their need to consider their options.
2. Offer to send a follow-up email summarizing your discussion and including your contact information.
3. Invite them to reach out if they have questions or decide to proceed in the future.
4. If appropriate, provide resources or referrals that might be helpful.

If the Client Decides to Schedule an Appointment

Before ending the call, be sure to take the following steps:

1. Schedule the first session, confirming the date and time.
2. Gather necessary information:
   - Confirm the spelling of the client's name.
   - Verify the email address they want to use for communication and portal access.
   - Collect any other essential details needed for your EHR system.
3. Explain the onboarding process:
   - Inform the client that you'll set them up in your electronic health record (EHR) system and client portal.

- Provide a timeline for when they'll receive access to the secure client portal.
- Explain that you will send intake forms through the portal for them to complete.
- Detail the intake forms they'll need to complete, emphasizing the importance of submitting these at least twenty-four to forty-eight hours before the appointment.
- Provide clear instructions on how to access and submit the forms through the portal.
- Offer assistance if they have questions about the forms or the process.
- Explain that accommodations are available for clients who may have difficulty with the intake process due to language barriers, cognitive impairments, or other challenges.

After the call, follow up with these steps:

1. Set up the client in your EHR system:
   - Create a new client profile using the verified information.
   - Generate portal access for the client.
2. Send intake forms through the secure client portal:
   - Demographic information form
   - Informed consent document
   - HIPAA privacy notice
   - Release of information form
   - Billing and payment agreement
   - Credit card authorization form
   - Good faith estimate (for clients paying out of pocket only)
   - Intake questionnaire or assessment

- Emergency contact information
- Telehealth consent form (if applicable)

3. Prepare your space:
   - Ensure your office (physical or virtual) is ready for the session.
   - Test any necessary technology or equipment.
   - Have any additional materials readily accessible.

4. Mental and emotional preparation:
   - Practice self-care techniques to ensure you're fully present and emotionally attuned for the first session.
   - Reflect on the client's initial goals or concerns mentioned during the consultation.
   - Review any intake forms or notes to familiarize yourself with the client's background.

Remember, this process aims to create a smooth, welcoming transition from the first point of contact to the beginning of the therapeutic relationship. With practice, you'll develop your own style and rhythm for these conversations, making them feel natural and tailored to each unique client interaction.

THE FIRST SESSION

The first session sets the foundation for the therapeutic relationship and establishes a safe and supportive environment for your client. It's an opportunity to build rapport, clarify expectations, and begin exploring the client's goals or concerns. Approaching the initial meeting with curiosity and empathy helps to create trust and sets the tone for a positive collaboration moving forward.

Reviewing Forms and Policies

At the start of the first session, take time to review the completed intake forms with the client. This process serves several important purposes: ensuring that the information provided is accurate and complete, clarifying any questions or concerns the client may have, and demonstrating your commitment to transparency and collaboration.

Begin by acknowledging the effort and vulnerability required to complete the intake forms and express appreciation for the client's willingness to share personal information. Invite the client to discuss any notable responses or discrepancies and encourage them to elaborate on their answers or ask questions. Pay particular attention to any sensitive or potentially traumatic experiences disclosed in the intake forms, and approach these topics with empathy, validation, and a nonjudgmental stance.

Use the intake information as a springboard to further explore the client's presenting concerns, treatment goals, and personal history. Ask open-ended questions that invite the client to share their perspective and fill in any gaps in the written responses. For example, you might ask, "In the intake form, you mentioned struggling with anxiety for several years. How would you say this has affected your daily life?" or "I noticed that you left the question about family mental health history blank. If you feel comfortable discussing this, how would you describe this history in your family?"

As you review the intake forms, note any inconsistencies, omissions, or areas that require further clarification. Gently probe for additional information while respecting the client's boundaries and right to privacy. If the client appears hesitant or uncomfortable discussing specific topics, acknowledge their feelings and reassure them that they can share at their own pace.

Next, explain your practice's privacy policies, including your obligations under HIPAA and any limits to confidentiality, such as mandated reporting requirements. Ensure the client understands their rights regarding access to their records, the use of their information for treatment, payment, and health care operations, such as billing, audits, and quality assessments, and the steps you take to protect their data. Review the informed consent document in detail, highlighting key points such as the nature of the therapeutic relationship, the anticipated course of treatment, and any potential risks or benefits. Obtain the client's signature acknowledging their understanding and agreement to participate in therapy.

Discuss the Release of Information form and the circumstances under which the client's PHI (protected health information) may be shared with others. Clarify the specific individuals or entities with whom the client has authorized communication, and explain the process for revoking or modifying this authorization if desired. Emphasize your commitment to protecting the client's privacy and only disclosing information when necessary and appropriate.

Addressing Financial Protocols

During the first session, it's essential to review the financial matters introduced in the consultation call and expand on them to ensure clarity and mutual understanding. This discussion reinforces transparency and helps both you and the client feel confident about moving forward in the therapeutic process.

Begin by confirming the fee structure, including the rates for initial assessments, ongoing sessions, and any additional services. Reference the consultation call as a reminder, saying, for example, "As we discussed in our initial call, the fee for a fifty-minute session is $175." If the client has expressed interest in a sliding scale or reduced fee, now is the time to review the eligibility criteria in detail and confirm any agreed-upon rate, if applicable.

For clients paying out of pocket, review the Good Faith Estimate provided earlier. Explain that this estimate, required by the No Surprises Act, outlines the expected charges for services over a period of time. Take a moment to address any questions or concerns the client may have about the estimate, ensuring they understand its purpose in preventing unexpected costs.

For clients using insurance, the specifics will vary depending on whether you're an in-network or out-of-network provider. For out-of-network services, remind the client they will be responsible for paying the full fee at the time of service. Confirm that you will provide them with a superbill to submit for reimbursement and encourage them to check with their insurance company about their out-of-network benefits. For in-network services, confirm the client's insurance coverage and benefits and clarify how the copayment or deductible will apply. Outline how you will bill their insurance and the portion of the fee they will be responsible for.

Next, outline the accepted payment methods, such as cash, check, credit card, or online payment platforms. Explain how clients can submit payment, whether at the time of service, through an invoice, or via automatic billing. If the client has provided a credit card authorization form with their intake paperwork, confirm the details and explain your procedures for using this card, whether for regular billing or for missed session fees. Ensure the client understands how their card information will be stored securely and used, and address any questions or concerns they may have.

Review your policies on missed sessions, late cancellations, and nonpayment. Explain any fees or charges associated with these situations, such as a percentage of the session fee for cancellations within a specific time frame. Clarify your expectations for rescheduling missed sessions, and discuss the consequences of repeated no-shows or late cancellations, reinforcing the importance of consistency in the therapeutic process.

Finally, provide contact information for any billing-related questions, and encourage the client to communicate any financial concerns or changes in their situation that might impact their ability to pay. Reassure them that you're willing to work with them to address any financial barriers that may arise during therapy.

By establishing clear, comprehensive financial protocols during the first session, you create a foundation of transparency, trust, and shared responsibility. This proactive approach helps to minimize financial stress or conflict, allowing both you and the client to focus on the meaningful work of therapy.

Discussing Scheduling

During the first session, it's essential to discuss scheduling with your client. Every therapist has their own approach that works best for their practice, and it's important to communicate this clearly.

Explain your scheduling system to the client. You might offer set weekly appointments, or you may prefer to schedule week-to-week at the end of each session. Some therapists use a combination of both methods, depending on client needs and practice management preferences.

Discuss the client's schedule, including any constraints or preferences they might have. Some clients have consistent availability, while others may have varying work hours or family commitments that require more flexibility.

If you offer different scheduling options, briefly explain each one. For set weekly appointments, highlight the benefits of consistency. For week-to-week scheduling, emphasize how it can accommodate changing schedules while maintaining regular therapy engagement.

Be clear about your own scheduling parameters, such as your working hours or how far in advance you book appointments. This helps set realistic expectations from the start.

Regardless of the method chosen, stress the importance of regular attendance for therapeutic progress. Encourage open communication about any attendance challenges that may arise.

Ultimately, the goal is to find a scheduling approach that supports the therapeutic process while being manageable for both you and your client. Clear communication about scheduling from the outset helps establish a foundation for a productive therapeutic relationship.

Explaining Communication Protocols

Effective communication is the cornerstone of a strong, productive therapeutic relationship. By establishing clear guidelines during the first meeting for communication between sessions, you help the client understand your availability, response times, and preferences for different modes of contact.

Begin by discussing your preferred methods for scheduling or canceling appointments, such as through your online client portal, by phone, or via email. Provide specific instructions for each method, such as the appropriate email address or phone number to use, and any relevant deadlines or cutoff times for making changes to the appointment schedule. Emphasize the importance of providing as much notice as possible for cancellations or rescheduling requests to enable you to offer the time slot to another client.

Next, explain your policies and procedures for handling client questions, concerns, or updates between sessions. Discuss the various modes of communication you offer, such as secure messaging through your client portal, encrypted email, or phone calls. Clarify your typical response times for each method, such as within twenty-four to forty-eight hours for nonurgent messages or within one business day for phone calls. Encourage the client to use the most appropriate mode of communication for their needs, taking into account factors such as the urgency and sensitivity of the information being shared.

Establish clear boundaries around the types of communication that are appropriate for different modes of contact. For example, you may specify that sensitive clinical information should only be shared through secure messaging or during scheduled sessions, while brief questions or scheduling requests can be handled via email or phone. Discuss any limitations on the length or frequency of between-session communication, such as a maximum number of messages per week or a time limit for phone calls.

Provide guidance on what constitutes an emergency or crisis situation that requires immediate attention, such as suicidal ideation, self-harm, or a significant deterioration in mental health symptoms. Explain how the client can access support or resources in these situations, such as by calling a crisis hotline, going to the nearest emergency room, or contacting you or another designated provider for urgent assistance. Ensure that the client has written copies of these emergency protocols and any relevant contact information.

Discuss your availability and boundaries around after-hours or weekend communication. Clarify whether you offer

24/7 emergency coverage or have specific hours during which you are available to respond to urgent needs. If you are part of a group practice or have coverage arrangements with other providers, explain how the client can access support outside your regular business hours.

Encourage the client to communicate openly and honestly about their experiences in therapy, including any concerns, questions, or feedback they may have about the therapeutic process or the working relationship. Emphasize that their input is valuable and essential for ensuring that therapy remains relevant, engaging, and effective. Invite the client to share their preferred communication style and any specific needs or accommodations they may have, such as a desire for more frequent check-ins or a preference for written communication due to hearing difficulties.

Finally, discuss any potential risks or limitations associated with electronic communication, such as the possibility of technical failures or privacy breaches. Provide guidance on how to minimize these risks, such as by using strong passwords, avoiding public Wi-Fi networks, and refraining from sharing sensitive information over unsecured channels. Obtain the client's consent to use electronic communication and document this agreement in their clinical record.

By establishing clear, comprehensive communication protocols and discussing them in detail during the first session, you create a foundation of transparency, responsiveness, and mutual understanding. This proactive approach helps to foster a sense of safety, trust, and collaboration, allowing the client to feel heard, supported, and empowered throughout their therapeutic journey.

NAVIGATING CHALLENGES

While we strive for smooth consultations and first sessions, it's important to be prepared for potential challenges. Common situations you might encounter include clients experiencing emotional distress, expressing resistance or skepticism about therapy, or having expectations that don't align with what you can offer. You may also face instances of boundary testing, cultural misunderstandings, technical difficulties in virtual sessions, or the disclosure of urgent issues requiring immediate attention.

When faced with a client in emotional distress, remain calm and empathetic. Validate their feelings and offer grounding techniques if needed. If the distress is severe, assess for safety and provide appropriate resources or referrals.

For clients who express doubts about therapy or seem resistant to the process, address their concerns openly and nondefensively. Explain the potential benefits of therapy and invite them to share their reservations.

If you realize the client's expectations don't align with what you can offer, address this directly. Clarify your approach and limitations, and if necessary, discuss potential referrals to better-suited providers.

When clients push professional boundaries, it's important to respond calmly and professionally. This may include situations such as clients frequently requesting to reschedule sessions, contacting you outside of agreed-upon hours, or disputing your policies on fees or cancellations. In these instances, to ensure clarity and consistency, respond by calmly and firmly restating your policies and the rationale behind them.

In cases of cultural misunderstandings, acknowledge the misstep openly, apologize if necessary, express your commitment to learning, and ask for clarification to avoid future misunderstandings.

For virtual consultations, have a backup plan in case of technical issues. Provide alternative contact methods and be prepared to reschedule if needed.

If a client discloses information that requires immediate attention, such as suicidal thoughts or abuse, be prepared to shift gears. Have crisis protocols and resources ready to address urgent needs.

Remember, how you handle challenges can set the tone for the entire therapeutic relationship. Approach difficulties with patience, professionalism, and a genuine desire to understand and help. Your ability to navigate these situations skillfully can turn potential obstacles into opportunities for building trust and rapport.

Building effective client relationships from the very first interaction is a critical component of a successful therapy practice. Throughout this chapter, we've explored the key strategies and considerations for mastering the initial stages of the therapeutic relationship, from conducting thorough consultation calls to establishing and communicating comprehensive policies and protocols.

By approaching these tasks with intention, transparency, and a commitment to collaboration, you create a safe, supportive environment that encourages client engagement, trust, and growth. Remember that each client brings their own unique needs, preferences, and challenges, and it's up to you to remain flexible, responsive, and attuned to their evolving needs.

As you continue to refine and adapt your approach to building client relationships, make sure to prioritize open communication, active listening, and a nonjudgmental stance. These elements foster a therapeutic alliance built on mutual respect, understanding, and a shared commitment to healing and growth.

REFLECT AND TAKE ACTION

In this chapter, we've explored the crucial components of building effective client relationships from the very first interaction. From conducting productive consultation calls to setting clear expectations and establishing comprehensive policies, the strategies discussed lay the foundation for a strong, trusting therapeutic alliance that can withstand the challenges of the healing process.

Key Takeaways
1. Effective consultation calls involve assessing the fit between therapist and client, actively listening to the client's concerns, and providing a clear overview of your therapeutic approach and philosophy.
2. Approach each client interaction with cultural humility and awareness, recognizing the impact of diverse backgrounds on the therapeutic process.
3. Transparency regarding fees and insurance is essential for building trust and preventing misunderstandings. Clearly communicate your rates, payment policies, and accepted insurance plans during the consultation call. Explain out-of-network benefits, if applicable, and discuss sliding scale options when appropriate.
4. Setting clear expectations about the structure, frequency, and duration of therapy, as well as the importance of regular attendance and active participation, helps clients understand their role in the therapeutic process and increases the likelihood of positive outcomes.

5. Thorough preparation for the first session, including creating a client profile, providing access to intake forms, and reviewing background information, demonstrates your professionalism and commitment to the client's well-being.

6. A comprehensive intake packet, including demographic information, informed consent, HIPAA privacy notice, and other essential forms, gathers the necessary information to develop an effective treatment plan and ensure compliance with legal and ethical standards.

7. Reviewing intake forms and policies during the first session ensures accuracy, clarifies questions, and demonstrates your commitment to transparency and collaboration. This includes discussing sensitive information with empathy and respect.

8. Establishing clear financial protocols, including fee structures, payment methods, and policies for missed sessions or nonpayment, helps maintain the stability and sustainability of your practice. This includes discussing options for clients concerned about affordability.

9. Be prepared to navigate common challenges in initial client interactions, such as emotional distress, resistance, or mismatched expectations.

10. Effective communication protocols, such as guidelines for scheduling, between-session contact, and emergency situations, foster a sense of safety, trust, and collaboration throughout the therapeutic journey. This includes setting clear boundaries for different types of communication.

11. Working collaboratively with clients to establish a consistent, predictable therapy schedule that

accommodates their needs and preferences helps minimize missed sessions and ensures they receive the support needed to achieve their goals.

12. Clearly outlining next steps after the consultation call, whether the client decides to proceed with therapy or not, demonstrates professionalism and care for the client's well-being.

Action Steps

1. Review and refine your consultation call process to ensure you are effectively assessing fit, actively listening to clients' concerns, and clearly communicating your therapeutic approach.

2. Develop strategies to enhance your cultural competence, including ongoing education and self-reflection on your own biases and assumptions.

3. Establish a comprehensive fee and insurance policy that clearly outlines your rates, accepted payment methods, and procedures for working with out-of-network benefits. Include information on sliding scale options if offered. Communicate this policy to potential clients during consultation calls.

4. Create a checklist of key points to discuss when setting expectations with new clients, including the structure of sessions, the importance of regular attendance, and your approach to tracking progress and adjusting treatment plans.

5. Streamline your first session preparation process by creating templates for client profiles, intake forms, and case files within your EHR system. Establish a timeline for clients to complete intake forms prior to the first session.

6. Review and update your intake packet to ensure it includes all necessary forms and documents, such as demographic information, informed consent, HIPAA privacy notice, and release of information. Ensure these forms are written in clear, accessible language.

7. Develop a protocol for reviewing intake forms and policies with clients during the first session, including strategies for addressing sensitive information, clarifying questions, and obtaining signatures.

8. Establish clear financial protocols for your practice, including fee structures, accepted payment methods, and policies for missed sessions or nonpayment. Include procedures for discussing financial concerns and exploring options for making therapy more accessible. Communicate these protocols to clients during the first session and obtain necessary agreements in writing.

9. Create guidelines for effective communication with clients, including preferred methods for scheduling, between-session contact, and emergency situations. Clearly outline boundaries for different types of communication, and discuss these protocols with clients during the first session. Provide written copies for their reference.

10. Create a protocol for handling common challenges in initial client interactions, including resources for crisis situations and referrals when needed.

11. Develop a process for collaboratively establishing therapy schedules with clients, taking into account their needs, preferences, and practical constraints.

12. Create a standardized process for following up after consultation calls, including procedures for clients

who decide to proceed with therapy and those who do not.

By implementing these key takeaways and action steps, you will be well-equipped to build strong, effective client relationships from the very first interaction. Remember, the therapeutic alliance is the foundation upon which all progress and healing is built. By investing time, energy, and care into these initial stages of the relationship, you set the stage for a transformative and rewarding journey for both you and your clients.

As we conclude this chapter on building effective client relationships, it's important to remember that your ability to provide exceptional care is directly linked to your own well-being. In the next chapter, we'll explore the critical topic of self-care and personal wellness for therapists. By prioritizing your own mental, emotional, and physical health, you'll be better equipped to navigate the challenges of client relationships and maintain a thriving, sustainable practice.

11

PRIORITIZING PERSONAL WELL-BEING FOR SUSTAINABLE SUCCESS

As a therapist, you pour your heart and soul into helping your clients navigate life's challenges and achieve their goals. Your work is deeply rewarding, but it can also be emotionally and mentally taxing. To build and maintain a thriving therapy practice, it is essential to recognize that your personal well-being is just as important as the well-being of your clients and the health of your business. Neglecting self-care can lead to imbalance, burnout, and ultimately, the deterioration of the very practice you've worked so hard to create.

In this chapter, we'll explore the critical importance of prioritizing your personal well-being as a therapist and practice owner. We'll discuss strategies for setting boundaries between work and personal life, dedicating quality time for self-care activities, and developing a supportive work environment aligned with your values. By proactively investing in your own well-being, you'll be better equipped to sustain the passion, presence, and effectiveness that are the hallmarks of a successful therapy practice.

THE RISKS OF NEGLECTING SELF-CARE

As a therapist, you are your most valuable resource. Your ability to be fully present, empathetic, and attuned to your clients' needs depends on your own emotional and mental well-being. When you neglect self-care, you risk becoming depleted, disengaged, and ultimately, ineffective in your work.

Burnout is a common and serious problem among mental health professionals. Characterized by emotional exhaustion, depersonalization, and a reduced sense of personal accomplishment, burnout can have devastating consequences for both therapists and their clients. Therapists experiencing burnout may feel drained and emotionally depleted, detached, or disillusioned, which can lead to a deterioration in the quality of care they provide. They may also experience physical symptoms such as fatigue, headaches, or digestive problems, as well as psychological symptoms such as anxiety, depression, or irritability.

The impact of burnout extends beyond the individual therapist to the practice as a whole. When a therapist is burned out, they may become less motivated, less productive, and less engaged in the growth and development of the practice. They may cancel sessions, fall behind on documentation, or make errors in clinical judgment. Over time, this can erode client trust, damage the practice's reputation, and undermine its financial stability.

To prevent burnout and maintain a sustainable, successful practice, it is essential to prioritize self-care and create a work environment that supports your personal well-being. This requires a proactive, intentional approach to setting boundaries, managing your workload, and investing in activities and relationships that nourish and replenish you.

SETTING BOUNDARIES BETWEEN WORK AND PERSONAL LIFE

One of the most important strategies for maintaining personal well-being as a therapist is setting clear boundaries between your work and personal life. When the lines between work and home become blurred, it can be difficult to fully relax, recharge, and engage in the activities and relationships that bring you joy and fulfillment.

To set effective boundaries, start by establishing dedicated work hours and communicating them clearly to your clients and colleagues. Let your clients know when you are available for sessions, phone calls, or email correspondence, and stick to those hours as much as possible. Use voice mail, email autoresponders, or other tools to communicate your availability and set expectations for response times.

It's also important to create a physical separation between your work and personal space, especially if you work from home. Designate a specific area of your home as your office, and avoid doing work in other areas such as your bedroom or living room. When you're not working, make a conscious effort to disconnect from work-related tasks and technology, such as turning off your phone and closing your email.

My own experience as a practice owner illustrates the importance of setting and maintaining these boundaries.

When I first started my private practice, I fell into the common trap of believing I had to accommodate every client's schedule to build a successful business. I worked with children, families, and couples, which meant offering evening hours to meet their needs. I set up a split schedule two days a week, seeing clients during the day, then leaving to pick up my kids and help with homework, only to return to work for a few more hours in the evening while a babysitter watched my children until their father got home.

I maintained this grueling schedule for about a year, even though it went against my personal preferences and the very reasons I had started a private practice in the first place. I didn't want to sacrifice evenings with my family, and I found the split schedule draining. But I convinced myself it was necessary to build my caseload and establish a thriving practice.

The reality was far from ideal. This demanding schedule led to burnout, and I began dreading the moments when I had to leave my children to return to work in the evenings. It starkly contradicted the work-life balance I had envisioned when I began my private practice journey.

After a year of this unsustainable routine, I realized something had to change. I began to phase out evening clients and transitioned to seeing clients only during school hours. Now I maintain firm boundaries around my working days and hours. This shift has been transformative, allowing me to feel energized throughout the week, month, and year. Most importantly, it aligns with my original goals for starting a private practice: achieving a fulfilling career while prioritizing my family and personal well-being.

This experience underscores the critical importance of aligning your practice with your personal values and priorities. While it may seem necessary to accommodate every client request when starting out, setting clear boundaries from the beginning can lead to a more sustainable and fulfilling practice in the long run.

In addition to setting boundaries around your time and space, it's important to set emotional boundaries as well. As a therapist, you may feel a strong sense of responsibility for your clients' well-being, but it's important to remember that you cannot control their choices or outcomes. Practice letting go of work-related stress and worry when you're not in session, and trust in your clients' resilience and ability to cope with life's challenges.

DEDICATING QUALITY TIME FOR SELF-CARE

Another key strategy for maintaining personal well-being is dedicating quality time for self-care activities and hobbies. Self-care looks different for everyone, but the goal is to engage in activities that bring you joy, relaxation, and a sense of fulfillment outside your work as a therapist.

Some examples of self-care activities might include

- exercise or physical activity, such as yoga, hiking, or dancing
- creative pursuits, such as painting, writing, or playing music
- spending time in nature, such as gardening or walking in the park
- connecting with loved ones, such as having dinner with friends or playing with your children
- engaging in spiritual or religious practices, such as meditation or prayer
- learning new skills or hobbies, such as cooking or photography

The key is to make self-care a regular, nonnegotiable part of your routine. Schedule self-care activities into your calendar just as you would a client session or a business meeting. Treat them as sacred, essential parts of your day, rather than optional extras that can be skipped when you're busy or stressed.

The following example from my coaching practice illustrates how crucial it is not just to acknowledge the importance of self-care but to be intentional about integrating it into one's daily routine.

I once worked with a therapist named Charlotte who found herself trapped in a cycle of burnout and exhaustion. Despite her best efforts, she felt constantly overworked, drained, and low on energy, regardless of how much sleep she got. Exercise, which had always been a source of rejuvenation for her, had fallen by the wayside. She would make excuses not to go to the gym after work, citing fatigue and overly hectic mornings due to family obligations. As a self-proclaimed "night owl," early morning workouts weren't an option either.

By not prioritizing her self-care or scheduling it into her day, she found herself caught in a vicious cycle. The less she exercised, the more exhausted she felt, which in turn made it even harder to find the motivation to work out. Her burnout deepened, and her overall well-being suffered.

During our work together, we explored her daily routine and values. It became clear that exercise wasn't just a luxury for her—it was a necessity for her mental and physical health. We brainstormed ways to incorporate it back into her life in a sustainable manner.

The breakthrough came when we restructured her daily schedule. Instead of trying to squeeze in a workout before or after her full day, we carved out time immediately after her last client session. This allowed her to go straight to the gym for an hour, reset her mind and body, and rejuvenate before transitioning to her family responsibilities.

This simple yet effective change made a world of difference. By making self-care through exercise a nonnegotiable part of her daily routine, she broke free from the cycle of excuses. It was no longer optional—it became as integral to her schedule as seeing clients or picking up her kids.

The results were transformative. Not only did she regain her energy and enthusiasm, but she also found herself more present and engaged with both her clients and her family. This experience underscored the critical importance of not just recognizing the need for self-care but actively prioritizing and scheduling it in a way that aligns with one's personal rhythms and responsibilities.

This therapist's journey highlights the transformative power of prioritizing self-care. By treating it as a nonnegotiable part of her schedule, she was able to break the cycle of burnout and rediscover her passion for her work and her life. Remember, self-care isn't selfish—it's an essential investment in your ability to show up fully for your clients and your loved ones.

It's also important to prioritize relationships and social connections outside your work as a therapist. Spending quality time with family, friends, and loved ones can provide a much-needed sense of support, perspective, and joy. Make an effort to nurture these relationships, even when your schedule is busy or you feel drained from work.

CREATING A SUPPORTIVE WORK ENVIRONMENT

In addition to setting boundaries and dedicating time for self-care, it's important to create a work environment that supports your personal well-being. This means aligning your practice with your values, managing your workload effectively, and creating a nurturing physical space.

Start by reflecting on your personal and professional values. What matters most to you in your work as a therapist? What kind of impact do you want to have on your clients and your community? Use these values as a guide for making decisions about your practice, from the clients you work with to the policies you put in place.

Next, take a proactive approach to managing your workload. This might involve setting limits on the number of clients you see each week, delegating administrative tasks to support staff, or outsourcing certain aspects of your practice, such as billing or marketing. It's also important to develop a routine for balancing client sessions with administrative tasks, such as scheduling, documentation, and continuing education.

To increase your focus and productivity, consider implementing techniques such as time blocking, pomodoro sessions (twenty-five-minute focused work intervals followed by five-minute breaks), or other time-management strategies. These tools can help you stay on track and avoid getting bogged down in distractions or low-priority tasks.

As the "CEO" of your practice, it's also important to schedule protected time for strategic planning and big-picture thinking. Set aside regular blocks of time to review your practice's performance, set goals, and make plans for growth and development. This might involve attending workshops or conferences, reading industry publications, or seeking guidance from mentors or consultants.

Finally, create a nurturing physical environment that supports your well-being and helps you feel centered and focused. This might involve decorating your office with calming colors and textures, incorporating plants or natural light, or investing in comfortable, ergonomic furniture. Consider adding elements that promote relaxation and mindfulness, such as a meditation cushion or a diffuser with essential oils.

RECOGNIZING AND PREVENTING BURNOUT

Even with the best self-care practices in place, it's important to remain vigilant for signs of burnout and take proactive steps to prevent it. Burnout is a state of emotional, mental, and physical exhaustion caused by prolonged stress and over-work. It can manifest in a variety of ways:

- Feeling constantly tired, drained, or overwhelmed
- Losing interest or motivation in your work
- Feeling cynical, irritable, or resentful toward clients or colleagues
- Experiencing physical symptoms such as headaches, digestive problems, or muscle tension
- Having difficulty concentrating, making decisions, or completing tasks
- Withdrawing from social connections or activities you once enjoyed

If you notice any of these warning signs in yourself, it's important to take action quickly to prevent burnout from taking hold. Start by conducting a self-assessment to identify areas of your work or personal life that may be contributing to your stress and exhaustion. Consider factors such as your workload, your boundaries, your self-care practices, and your support system.

Based on your assessment, develop a plan for managing burnout and improving your well-being. This might involve any or a combination of the following:

- Adjusting your workload or schedule to allow for more rest and recovery time

- Delegating or outsourcing tasks that are draining or overwhelming
- Seeking support from colleagues, mentors, or a therapist of your own
- Recommitting to your self-care practices and making them a nonnegotiable part of your routine
- Setting stronger boundaries around your time, energy, and emotional availability
- Engaging in activities that promote relaxation, joy, and creativity

It's also important to build a strong support system of peers and colleagues who understand the unique challenges and rewards of therapy work. Consider joining a professional organization, attending workshops or retreats, or participating in online forums or discussion groups. These connections can provide valuable perspective, advice, and encouragement when you're feeling stuck or burned out.

CONTINUALLY INVESTING IN YOUR OWN GROWTH

Finally, prioritizing your personal well-being means continually investing in your own growth and self-work. As a therapist, you are a lifelong learner, constantly evolving and expanding your knowledge and skills. By committing to your own personal and professional development, you not only improve your ability to serve your clients but also deepen your sense of purpose and fulfillment in your work.

Here are some ways to invest in your own growth:

- Attending workshops, conferences, or training programs to learn new therapeutic techniques or approaches

- Pursuing advanced degrees or certifications in your field
- Engaging in your own therapy to process personal challenges or blind spots
- Practicing mindfulness, meditation, or other self-reflection techniques
- Reading books, articles, or research on topics related to your work or personal interests
- Seeking feedback or guidance from mentors, supervisors, or peers
- Experimenting with new hobbies or creative pursuits that challenge and inspire you

By continually learning, growing, and exploring new horizons, you keep your work fresh, engaging, and meaningful. You model for your clients the kind of curiosity, openness, and resilience that are essential for personal and professional growth.

Building and maintaining a successful therapy practice requires more than clinical skills and business savvy. It requires a deep commitment to one's own well-being and a willingness to prioritize self-care, boundaries, and growth. By nurturing all the elements of your practice, including one's own physical, emotional, and mental health, one creates a sustainable foundation for long-term success and fulfillment.

Remember, taking care of yourself is not selfish or indulgent. It is an essential part of your work as a therapist and a practice owner. When you show up for yourself with compassion, patience, and dedication, you are better equipped to show up for your clients and your business with the same level of presence, skill, and heart.

As you continue on your journey as a therapist and practice owner, make self-care a nonnegotiable part of your routine.

Set boundaries that protect your time and energy, both at work and at home. Dedicate quality time to activities and relationships that nourish and replenish you. Create a work environment that supports your well-being and aligns with your values. And always, always keep learning, growing, and investing in your own personal and professional development.

By prioritizing your personal well-being, you not only build a thriving, successful practice but also model for your clients and your community what it means to live a life of purpose, balance, and joy. You become a beacon of hope and healing, not just through your words and techniques but through your very presence and way of being in the world. And that, in the end, is the greatest gift you can give to your-self, your clients, and your practice.

REFLECT AND TAKE ACTION

In this chapter, we've explored the importance of prior-itizing personal well-being for the long-term success and sustainability of your therapy practice. We've discussed the risks of neglecting self-care, the strategies for setting bound-aries and creating a supportive work environment, the impor-tance of recognizing and preventing burnout, and the value of continually investing in your own growth and development.

Key Takeaways
- Neglecting self-care can lead to burnout, imbalance, and the deterioration of your practice. Prioritizing your personal well-being is essential for maintaining the passion, presence, and effectiveness that are the hallmarks of a successful therapist and practice owner.
- Setting clear boundaries between work and personal life is crucial for preventing overwork and allowing

time for rest, relaxation, and self-care. This includes establishing dedicated work hours, creating a physical separation between work and home, and setting emotional boundaries around your responsibility for client outcomes.

- Dedicating quality time for self-care activities, hobbies, and relationships outside work is essential for maintaining balance, joy, and perspective. Treat self-care as a nonnegotiable part of your routine, and prioritize activities that bring you relaxation, fulfillment, and connection.

- Creating a supportive work environment that aligns with your values and promotes your well-being is key to long-term success. This includes managing your workload effectively, implementing strategies for focus and productivity, scheduling time for strategic planning, and creating a nurturing physical space.

- Recognizing and preventing burnout requires vigilance, self-awareness, and proactive self-care. Conduct regular self-assessments, seek support from colleagues and mentors, and take swift action to address warning signs of emotional, mental, or physical exhaustion.

- Continually investing in your own personal and professional growth is essential for maintaining passion, skill, and relevance in your work. Pursue learning opportunities, engage in your own therapy or self-reflection, and seek feedback and guidance from trusted peers and mentors.

Action Steps

1. Conduct a self-assessment of your current self-care practices and the overall health of your practice. Identify areas where you need to set stronger

boundaries, make more time for self-care, or create a more supportive work environment.

2. Choose one or two specific self-care activities that you will commit to incorporating into your regular routine. Schedule them into your calendar and treat them as nonnegotiable priorities.

3. Review your workload and identify areas where you can delegate, outsource, or streamline tasks to create more space for focus, productivity, and strategic planning. Implement at least one strategy for improving your time management and reducing stress.

4. Assess your current support system of colleagues, mentors, and professional communities. Identify opportunities for deepening your connections, seeking guidance, or collaborating with others who share your values and challenges.

5. Choose one area of personal or professional growth that you will prioritize in the coming months. This might include attending a workshop, pursuing a certification, or starting a new self-reflection practice. Create a plan for how you will incorporate this learning into your work and life.

6. Review the warning signs of burnout and create a personalized plan for recognizing and addressing them in yourself. Share your plan with a trusted colleague or mentor who can support you in maintaining accountability and taking action when needed.

By implementing these key takeaways and action steps, you'll be building a more sustainable, fulfilling, and successful therapy practice. Remember, prioritizing your own well-being is not a selfish act but rather an essential foundation for serving your clients and growing your business with passion, skill, and heart.

As you implement these strategies for prioritizing your personal well-being, it's important to remember that the path to a thriving practice is not always smooth. Challenges and obstacles are an inevitable part of any professional journey. In the next chapter, we'll explore how to overcome these hurdles and build the resilience necessary to navigate the ups and downs of owning and operating a therapy practice. By combining a strong foundation of self-care with effective strategies for facing adversity, you'll have the tools you need to build a practice that can weather any storm and emerge stronger on the other side.

12

OVERCOMING OBSTACLES AND BUILDING RESILIENCE

As a therapist in private practice, you have the incredible opportunity to make a profound difference in the lives of your clients. However, this rewarding path is not without its challenges. From navigating the complexities of clinical work to managing the demands of running a business, you'll encounter various obstacles that can test your resolve and shake your confidence.

In this chapter, we'll explore these common challenges and provide you with practical strategies for overcoming them. We'll begin by addressing one of the most pervasive issues faced by therapists: impostor syndrome. You'll learn effective techniques for reframing negative self-talk, seeking support, and cultivating a growth mindset.

We'll then discuss other key challenges, such as managing client expectations, dealing with difficult cases, and maintaining professional growth. Throughout, we'll emphasize the importance of building emotional resilience and creating a supportive professional environment.

By the end of this chapter, you'll be equipped with a tool kit of practical strategies for navigating obstacles and building a thriving, fulfilling private practice. Remember, every challenge you face is an opportunity for growth and learning. With the right mindset and tools, you can overcome any obstacle and create a practice that truly makes a difference.

UNDERSTANDING AND OVERCOMING IMPOSTOR SYNDROME

Impostor syndrome is a pervasive psychological phenomenon that affects countless professionals, and therapists in private practice are no exception. It's characterized by a persistent belief that one's successes are due to luck or external factors rather than one's own abilities and hard work. Despite evidence of their competence and achievements, individuals struggling with impostor syndrome often feel like frauds, constantly fearing they'll be exposed as unqualified or undeserving of their position.

For therapists in private practice, impostor syndrome can manifest in both clinical and business aspects of their work. In the clinical realm, you might find yourself questioning your ability to help clients effectively, doubting your skills and expertise. You may compare yourself unfavorably to colleagues, feeling like you don't measure up or you lack the necessary qualifications to provide high-quality care. Even when clients express gratitude and make progress, you might attribute these successes to factors outside your own abilities.

On the business side, impostor syndrome can lead you to doubt your entrepreneurial skills and your capacity to build and maintain a successful practice. You might question your ability to market your services, attract clients, and manage the financial and administrative aspects of running a business. The fear of being exposed as a "fraud" can lead to anxiety, procrastination, and a reluctance to take risks or seize opportunities for growth.

To illustrate the impact of impostor syndrome, let's consider the example of Dr. Sarah, a talented and experienced therapist who recently started her own private practice. Despite her years of training and track record of helping clients achieve positive outcomes, Dr. Sarah constantly worries that she's not good enough. She second-guesses her clinical decisions, spends hours overpreparing for sessions, and feels guilty about charging for her services. When a client thanks her for a particularly insightful session, she brushes off the compliment, thinking, "Oh, I just got lucky today. I'm not really that skilled."

Dr. Sarah's impostor syndrome also affects her business growth. She struggles to promote her practice, fearing that she'll be exposed as an impostor if she puts herself out there. She hesitates to network with other professionals or pursue speaking engagements, worried that others will see through her façade and realize she's not as knowledgeable as she appears. As a result, her practice grows slowly, and she misses out on opportunities to share her expertise and help more people.

Fortunately, there are effective strategies that therapists like Dr. Sarah can use to overcome impostor syndrome and build a thriving, fulfilling private practice. Below are five key approaches.

1. **Reframing negative self-talk:** One of the most powerful tools for combating impostor syndrome is learning to recognize and reframe the negative self-talk that fuels it. When thoughts like *I'm not good enough* or *I don't deserve this success* arise, take a step back and challenge them. Ask yourself, *What evidence do I have to support this belief?* and *What would I say to a colleague or friend who expressed similar doubts?*

Practice replacing these negative thoughts with more balanced, compassionate statements that acknowledge your skills and achievements.

2. **Seeking support and mentorship:** Impostor syndrome can be incredibly isolating, making it feel like you're the only one struggling with these doubts. Reaching out to trusted colleagues, mentors, or a therapist of your own can help you gain perspective and realize you're not alone. Seek out supportive relationships where you can share your experiences, receive guidance, and celebrate your successes together.

3. **Celebrating successes and learning from challenges:** When impostor syndrome strikes, it's easy to dismiss your accomplishments and dwell on your perceived failures or shortcomings. Make a conscious effort to acknowledge and celebrate your successes, no matter how small they may seem. Keep a journal or a "brag file" where you record positive feedback, milestones, and moments of pride. At the same time, embrace challenges and setbacks as opportunities for growth and learning rather than as evidence of your inadequacy.

4. **Embracing a growth mindset:** Cultivating a growth mindset is essential for overcoming impostor syndrome and building confidence in your abilities. Recognize that your skills and knowledge are not fixed but can be developed and expanded through dedication, effort, and a willingness to learn. Embrace opportunities for professional development, whether through continuing education, workshops, or consultation with colleagues. Remember that growth and mastery are ongoing processes and that setbacks are a natural part of the journey.

5. **Practicing self-compassion and self-care:** Finally, be kind and compassionate with yourself. Recognize that impostor syndrome is a common experience and that struggling with self-doubt does not diminish your worth or competence as a therapist. Treat yourself with the same understanding and empathy that you would extend to a client or a beloved friend. Prioritize self-care practices that nourish your mind, body, and spirit, whether that's engaging in hobbies, spending time in nature, or connecting with supportive loved ones. Remember that taking care of yourself is not selfish, but essential for sustaining your ability to show up fully for your clients and your business.

By implementing these strategies consistently and compassionately, you can gradually chip away at impostor syndrome and build a stronger sense of self-efficacy and resilience. It's a process that requires patience, self-reflection, and a commitment to your own growth and well-being, but the rewards— both personally and professionally—are immeasurable. With time and practice, you can learn to embrace your unique strengths, celebrate your achievements, and show up with confidence and authenticity in your work as a therapist and private practice owner.

As you work to overcome impostor syndrome, remember that this journey is part of your professional growth. Every step you take toward building confidence in your abilities not only benefits you but also enhances the quality of care you provide to your clients. By addressing your own self-doubts, you're modeling resilience and self-compassion—valuable skills that you can then share with those you serve in your practice.

IDENTIFYING AND NAVIGATING OTHER COMMON CHALLENGES

While impostor syndrome is a significant challenge for many therapists in private practice, it is by no means the only one. As you navigate the complexities of clinical work and business ownership, you may encounter a range of other obstacles that can impact your professional growth, well-being, and success. Let's explore some of these common challenges and discuss strategies for effectively navigating them.

Managing Client Expectations

Managing client expectations is often one of the first hurdles therapists face in private practice. Clients come to therapy with a wide range of expectations, some of which may be unrealistic or misaligned with the therapeutic process. It's essential to communicate clearly what therapy can and cannot achieve and to collaborate with clients in setting realistic goals. Consider developing an intake process that includes a discussion of expectations and provides psycho-education about the nature of therapy and the client's role in the process. By setting clear boundaries and expectations from the outset, you can help prevent misunderstandings and foster a more productive therapeutic relationship.

Dealing with Difficult Cases

Dealing with difficult cases is another challenge that all therapists face at some point in their careers. As you build your practice, you will inevitably work with clients who present complex or challenging issues, such as personality disorders, trauma, or suicidal ideation. These cases can be emotionally taxing and may require specialized skills and knowledge. It's crucial to seek out ongoing training and consultation to build your competence in working with these populations. Engage in regular supervision or peer consultation to process challenging cases and receive guidance and support. Remember, it's okay to acknowledge your limitations and refer clients to specialists when necessary.

Maintaining Professional Growth

Maintaining professional growth can be challenging amid the demands of running a practice. Staying current with the latest research, theories, and techniques is essential for providing high-quality care to your clients. However, finding time for professional development can be difficult when you're juggling client sessions, administrative tasks, and personal responsibilities. Set aside dedicated time each week for learning activities, such as reading professional journals, attending webinars, or participating in online courses. Consider joining professional organizations and attending conferences to network with colleagues and learn from experts in the field. By prioritizing your own growth, you'll not only enhance your clinical skills but also stay energized and engaged in your work.

Handling the Emotional Impact of Therapy Work

Bearing witness to clients' pain, struggles, and traumatic experiences can take a significant toll on your own emotional well-being. This challenge, often referred to as vicarious trauma or compassion fatigue, can lead to burnout if not addressed proactively. It's crucial to recognize the signs of emotional strain and develop strategies to protect your mental health. While we'll explore building emotional resilience in more depth later in this chapter, remember that prioritizing self-care and seeking support when needed are essential components of maintaining your effectiveness as a therapist.

Navigating Billing and Financial Issues

Navigating billing and financial issues can be one of the most daunting aspects of running a private practice. Managing the financial aspects of your business can be complex and time-consuming, especially when dealing with insurance reimbursement, client payments, and book-keeping. To streamline these processes, consider investing in practice management software that includes features for billing, invoicing, and financial tracking. Seek out resources and training on financial management for therapists, and consider working with a bookkeeper or accountant who specializes in mental health practices. By getting a handle on the financial side of your practice, you'll reduce stress and have more energy to focus on your clinical work.

Managing a Busy Caseload and Scheduling

As your practice grows, managing a busy caseload and scheduling can become increasingly challenging. You may find yourself juggling a high volume of clients and a packed schedule, leaving little time for self-care or professional development. It's important to set realistic boundaries around your availability and to prioritize time for your own needs. If necessary, consider implementing more stringent policies for cancellations, rescheduling, and between-session contact to manage client expectations and protect your time. Use scheduling tools and virtual assistants to streamline appointment booking and reduce administrative tasks. Remember, it's okay to have a waiting list or to refer clients to other therapists if your caseload becomes unmanageable.

Staying Compliant with Laws, Regulations, and Ethical Guidelines

Finally, staying compliant with laws, regulations, and ethical guidelines is an ongoing challenge for therapists in private practice. As a mental health professional, you are bound by a complex web of legal and ethical obligations. Staying up-to-date with changing laws, regulations, and best practices is essential for protecting your clients' well-being and your own professional standing. Regularly review updates from professional organizations, licensing boards, and health care authorities. Attend workshops or consult with legal experts to ensure that your practice is fully compliant with HIPAA, state laws, and ethical standards. While navigating these requirements can be complex, remember that they exist to protect both you and your clients.

Building Challenges and Growing Professionally

By acknowledging these common challenges and developing strategies to address them, you can build a more resilient and successful private practice. Remember that facing obstacles is a natural part of professional growth, and each challenge you overcome strengthens your skills and confidence as a therapist and business owner. As you navigate these hurdles, draw on the support of colleagues, mentors, and professional resources. With patience, perseverance, and a commitment to ongoing learning, you can overcome these challenges and create a thriving, fulfilling private practice.

As we've explored these common challenges, you may have noticed a recurring theme: the importance of resilience and a supportive environment in navigating the complexities of private practice. While each challenge requires specific strategies, your overall ability to thrive in the face of these obstacles depends largely on your emotional resilience and the support systems you create. Let's now turn our attention to building these crucial foundations that will underpin your success in addressing all the challenges we've discussed.

BUILDING EMOTIONAL RESILIENCE AND CREATING A SUPPORTIVE ENVIRONMENT

As you navigate the challenges of private practice, you'll quickly discover that success requires more than just clinical expertise and business acumen. It demands a deep well of emotional resilience—the ability to adapt to adversity, bounce back from setbacks, and maintain a sense of purpose in the face of uncertainty. Equally important is the creation of a supportive professional environment that nurtures your growth and sustains your passion for the work.

Cultivating resilience begins with embracing a growth mindset. Rather than viewing challenges as threats or failures, approach them with curiosity and openness. Each difficult case, each business setback, becomes an opportunity to learn and develop. This mindset builds confidence in your ability to adapt and thrive in the face of change and adversity.

Developing Your Stress Management Tool Kit

A crucial aspect of building resilience is developing effective strategies to manage the stress and emotional impact of therapy work. This is particularly important given the potential for vicarious trauma and compassion fatigue we discussed earlier. Your stress management tool kit should include techniques for both immediate relief and long-term emotional well-being.

Consider incorporating some of the following practices:

1. Mindfulness and meditation—These can help you stay grounded and present, even when dealing with challenging client material.
2. Regular physical exercise—This can help reduce stress and improve overall mental health.
3. Creative outlets—Engaging in art, music, or writing can provide emotional release and processing.
4. Professional boundaries—Establish clear limits between work and personal life to prevent emotional spillover.
5. Debriefing—Regularly process complex cases with a supervisor or trusted colleague.
6. Personal therapy—Engaging in your own therapy can help you process your experiences and maintain emotional balance.

Make these practices a nonnegotiable part of your routine, as essential to your professional success as any clinical skill. Remember, taking care of yourself isn't selfish—it's necessary for providing the best possible care to your clients and sustaining a long, fulfilling career in private practice.

Surrounding Yourself with Supportive Relationships

Remember, too, that resilience isn't built in isolation. It flourishes within a network of supportive relationships, both personal and professional. Cultivate connections with family and friends who can offer emotional support and a listening ear when the pressures of practice feel overwhelming. These relationships remind you that your worth extends far beyond your role as a therapist, helping you maintain a healthy perspective on your work.

Creating a Nurturing Professional Environment

In your professional life, seek out opportunities for connection and growth. Consider joining or forming a peer support group with other therapists in private practice. These groups can be invaluable sources of validation, resource sharing, and mutual encouragement. They provide a safe space to process complex cases, celebrate successes, and navigate the unique challenges of running a therapy business.

Valuing Ongoing Supervision and Consultation

Regular supervision or consultation is another cornerstone of a supportive professional environment. Even if you're no longer required to participate in supervision by your licensing board, engaging with a seasoned therapist can enhance your clinical skills, help you process countertransference, and identify blind spots in your practice. Look for a supervisor or consultation group that aligns with your theoretical orientation and professional goals.

Embracing Lifelong Learning

As you build your support network, embrace a mindset of lifelong learning. The mental health field constantly evolves, with new research, theories, and techniques emerging. Commit to ongoing professional development, whether through reading journals, attending workshops and conferences, or pursuing additional certifications. This continuous learning enhances your clinical effectiveness and keeps your work fresh and engaging, protecting against burnout.

Creating a Nurturing Physical Space

Consider, too, the physical environment of your practice. Create a space that reflects your values and promotes well-being for your clients and yourself. This might mean investing in comfortable, calming decor, ensuring good lighting and ventilation, or incorporating elements of nature into your office. A nurturing physical space can significantly impact your daily work experience and contribute to your overall resilience.

Embracing the Ongoing Journey of Resilience

Finally, remember that building resilience and creating a supportive environment is an ongoing process, not a one-time achievement. It requires consistent effort, self-reflection, and a willingness to adapt as your needs and circumstances change. Be patient with yourself as you navigate this journey. Celebrate your progress, learn from setbacks, and always hold on to the passion that brought you to this work in the first place.

The Role of Emotional Resilience in Private Practice

By intentionally cultivating emotional resilience and surrounding yourself with support, you lay the foundation for a thriving, sustainable private practice. You'll be better equipped to handle the challenges that come your way, maintain your enthusiasm for the work, and continue making a meaningful difference in your clients' lives for years to come.

Throughout this chapter, we've explored the myriad challenges that therapists face when building and maintaining a private practice. From the internal struggle of impostor syndrome to the practical hurdles of managing a business, each obstacle presents an opportunity for growth and development.

The key to thriving in private practice lies not just in addressing individual challenges but in cultivating a foundation of emotional resilience and a supportive professional environment. By embracing a growth mindset, developing effective stress management techniques, and creating a support network, you'll be better equipped to navigate whatever difficulties arise.

Remember, your journey in private practice is ongoing. Each challenge you face is an opportunity to refine your skills, deepen your understanding, and strengthen your resolve. Stay connected to your passion for helping others, and don't forget to extend the same compassion to yourself that you offer your clients.

As you move forward, carry with you the strategies and insights we've discussed. With persistence, self-reflection, and a commitment to ongoing growth, you can build a practice that not only weathers challenges but flourishes in the face of them. Your dedication to your clients, your profession, and your own development will guide you toward a fulfilling and impactful career in private practice.

REFLECT AND TAKE ACTION

Throughout this chapter, we've explored the various challenges therapists face when starting and growing a private practice, from impostor syndrome and managing client expectations to personal and administrative hurdles. We've discussed strategies for overcoming these obstacles, building emotional resilience, and creating a support system.

Key Takeaways
- Impostor syndrome is a common struggle among therapists in private practice, affecting both clinical and business aspects of the work. Overcoming it requires reframing negative self-talk, seeking support and mentorship, celebrating successes, and cultivating a growth mindset.

- Therapists face a range of other challenges, including managing client expectations, dealing with complex cases, maintaining professional growth, handling the emotional impact of the work, navigating billing and financial issues, managing a busy caseload and scheduling, and staying compliant with laws and regulations.
- Building emotional resilience is crucial for thriving in private practice. This involves embracing a growth mindset, developing stress-management techniques, prioritizing ongoing education and professional development, engaging in supervision or peer consultation, building a strong support network, and creating a nurturing physical workspace.
- Creating a supportive professional environment is essential for long-term success and well-being. This includes embracing a mindset of lifelong learning, attending workshops and conferences, and pursuing additional certifications or specializations.

Action Steps

1. Develop a personalized plan for addressing impostor syndrome. Identify your negative self-talk patterns and practice reframing techniques. Set aside time each week to celebrate your successes, no matter how small, and actively seek out supportive colleagues and mentors.
2. Create a "Challenge Action Plan." Identify the top three challenges you currently face or anticipate facing in your practice. For each challenge, outline specific steps you can take to address it, incorporating the strategies discussed in this chapter. Set realistic timelines for implementing these steps, and schedule regular check-ins to assess your progress.

3. Conduct a "Resilience Audit." Assess your current level of emotional resilience and identify areas for improvement. Develop a comprehensive self-care plan that includes regular stress-management practices. Schedule these activities into your weekly routine and treat them as nonnegotiable appointments with yourself.

4. Map your professional support network. Evaluate your existing professional connections and identify gaps or areas for growth. Research and reach out to at least one new resource each month, whether it's joining a peer support group, finding a mentor, or enrolling in a continuing education program that aligns with your interests and goals.

5. Assess your practice's physical environment. Identify ways to make your workspace more calming, comfortable, and conducive to your and your clients' well-being. Implement at least one improvement in the next month.

By implementing these key takeaways and action steps, you will take significant steps toward creating a more resilient, fulfilling, and successful therapy practice. Remember, building a thriving practice is a journey filled with both challenges and triumphs. Equipping yourself with the strategies and mindset outlined in this chapter allows you to navigate obstacles with greater confidence, adaptability, and resilience.

Embrace the process of continual growth and learning, and trust in your ability to make a profound difference in your clients' lives. You have the strength, wisdom, and dedication to overcome any challenge that comes your way. Believe in yourself and the transformative power of the work you do. Your commitment to your clients and your own personal and professional growth will lead you to a rewarding and meaningful journey in private practice.

As you implement these strategies and build your resilience, you'll be well-prepared for the next phase of your journey: sustaining your success and nurturing continued growth. In the final chapter, "Sustaining Success and Nurturing Growth," we'll explore how to maintain your momentum, expand your practice, and ensure long-term fulfillment in your career as a therapist in private practice.

13

SUSTAINING SUCCESS AND NURTURING GROWTH

Congratulations on launching your private practice! The knowledge and strategies you've gained from this book have equipped you with a solid foundation. However, your professional journey is just beginning. This final chapter serves as a strategic guide for the next phase: sustaining and growing the practice you've worked diligently to establish.

In the following pages, we'll explore methods to maintain your entrepreneurial drive and discuss advanced strategies to elevate your business. You'll discover ways to expand your professional influence beyond individual therapy sessions, potentially venturing into new territories such as public speaking, writing, or consulting.

Central to this chapter—and your ongoing success—is a focus on personal and professional development. We'll examine how continuous learning and growth are essential not only for the longevity of your practice but also for your own fulfillment and satisfaction in your work.

The skills and insights you've acquired are powerful tools. Here, we'll discuss how to leverage them effectively, creating a practice that succeeds in the present and continually evolves and thrives in the future.

As we review the strategies for sustaining success and fostering growth, remember that each step forward builds upon the strong foundation you've already created. Your journey as a private practitioner is unique, and the path ahead is filled with potential for both professional achievement and personal satisfaction.

EMBRACING THE TRANSFORMATIVE JOURNEY

When you first decided to establish your private practice, you likely experienced a mix of excitement and trepidation. While enticing, the prospect of running your own business can also be overwhelming. This transition from clinician to entrepreneur is a significant undertaking that requires a fundamental shift in how you perceive yourself and your work.

As you've progressed through this book, you've begun to embrace the dual role of healer and business owner. This duality is not a conflict but a powerful synergy that drives your success. Your clinical skills and empathy form the core of your practice, while your newfound business skills provide the structure and sustainability necessary for long-term success.

Throughout your journey, you've explored and internalized several core concepts that form the foundation of a thriving private practice. Let's revisit these concepts and consider how they've transformed your approach to your work.

First, you've cultivated an entrepreneurial mindset. This shift in perspective allows you to see opportunities where others might only see obstacles. You've learned to value innovation and calculated risk-taking, understanding that growth often requires stepping out of your comfort zone. This mindset also emphasizes the importance of continuous learning and adaptation, essential skills in the ever-evolving field of mental health care.

Financial empowerment has been another crucial area of development. You've gained a deeper understanding of the financial aspects of running a practice, from setting appropriate fees to managing cash flow. You've begun to think long-term, planning for your financial security and the sustainable growth of your practice.

Effective messaging has become a cornerstone of your practice's success. You've honed your ability to communicate your unique value proposition, crafting compelling messages that resonate with your ideal clients. This skill helps attract the right clients and sets you apart from other therapists. You've learned to articulate what makes your approach unique and how to best serve your target population.

Practice management, once perhaps an intimidating aspect of running your own business, has become second nature. You've mastered the operational aspects of running a practice, from efficient scheduling and client management to ensuring legal compliance and upholding ethical standards. These skills allow your practice to run smoothly, freeing up more time and energy to focus on what you do best: helping your clients.

Perhaps most importantly, you've built emotional resilience. The path of an entrepreneur is rarely smooth, and you've learned to navigate the inevitable challenges and setbacks with grace and determination. This resilience helps you persevere through difficult times and models healthy coping strategies for your clients.

As you reflect on these core concepts, it's important to recognize that they are not isolated skills or knowledge areas. Instead, they are interconnected pillars that support the structure of your thriving practice. Your entrepreneurial mindset informs your financial decisions and shapes your messaging strategy. Effective practice management ensures you can deliver on the promises made in your marketing, while your resilience enables you to persist and grow even when faced with obstacles.

Consider how these elements work together in your daily practice. Your entrepreneurial spirit might lead you to identify an underserved niche in your community. Your financial knowledge helps you determine how to price your services competitively while ensuring profitability. Your messaging skills allow you to effectively communicate the value of your specialized services to potential clients. Your practice management expertise ensures you can efficiently schedule and manage this new client base. And when challenges arise—as they inevitably will—your resilience keeps you moving forward, learning and adapting along the way.

This transformative journey from clinician to entrepreneur is ongoing. As you continue to grow and evolve as a private practitioner, these foundational concepts will continue to serve you. They provide a framework for decision-making, a guide for overcoming challenges, and a road map for future growth.

As we move forward in this chapter, we'll build upon these concepts, exploring strategies for sustaining your success and nurturing continued growth. Remember, the skills and knowledge you've gained are not static—they are dynamic tools that will continue to evolve as you and your practice grow. Embrace this ongoing transformation, celebrating how far you've come while looking forward to more exciting possibilities.

STAYING INNOVATIVE AND PROACTIVE

As a private practice owner, it's essential to maintain a proactive and innovative approach to ensure your business's long-term success and growth. In a rapidly evolving industry like mental health care, complacency can be detrimental to your practice's viability. To stay ahead of the curve and continue thriving, consider implementing the following strategies.

Setting New Business Goals on a Regular Basis

Setting new business goals is a crucial aspect of staying innovative and proactive. By continually establishing fresh objectives, you create a sense of forward momentum and prevent stagnation. These goals should be specific, measurable, achievable, relevant, and time-bound (SMART). Consider setting goals in various areas of your practice:

- Financial targets—Aim to increase revenue by a specific percentage or dollar amount within a defined time frame.
- Client acquisition—Set targets for attracting new clients, either through referrals, marketing efforts, or expansion of your service offerings.
- Professional development—Commit to attending a certain number of conferences, workshops, or training sessions each year to enhance your skills and knowledge.
- Operational efficiency—Identify areas of your practice that can be streamlined or automated to save time and resources.
- For example, Kathleen, a therapist who had been in private practice for five years, set a goal to expand her services to include group therapy sessions. She researched the demand for group therapy in her area, developed a marketing plan, and successfully launched her first group within six months. This targeted approach allowed her to expand her services and reach a new clientele.

By regularly setting and working toward new goals, you maintain a focus on continuous improvement and growth.

Staying Updated with Industry Trends

Staying informed about the latest trends, research, and best practices in the mental health field is essential for staying innovative and relevant. Commit to dedicating time each week or month to staying updated on industry developments.

Some strategies for staying informed include

- subscribing to professional journals and newsletters in your field of specialization
- attending conferences and workshops to learn about new treatment approaches, technologies, and business strategies
- participating in online forums and discussion groups to engage with colleagues and share ideas
- following thought leaders and influencers on social media to stay attuned to emerging trends and conversations

By staying updated on industry trends, you can identify opportunities to differentiate your practice, implement new treatment modalities, or improve your business operations.

Reassess Your Business Plan Periodically

Your business plan is a living document that should evolve as your practice grows and changes. Regularly reassessing and updating your business plan helps you stay proactive and adapt to new challenges and opportunities.

Set aside time annually or semiannually to review your business plan and consider the following factors:

- Changes in your local market or target clientele
- Emerging competitors or industry disruptors
- New technologies or treatment approaches that could impact your practice
- Shifts in your own goals, values, or priorities as a practitioner and business owner

Based on your assessment, make necessary adjustments to your business plan, such as refining your target market, updating your marketing strategies, or revising your financial projections.

By periodically reassessing your business plan, you can ensure that your practice remains aligned with your goals and responsive to changes in the industry. Implementing these strategies for staying innovative and proactive will help you maintain a competitive edge and continue growing your practice. Remember, the key is to embrace change and continuously seek out opportunities for improvement. By staying attuned to industry trends, regularly setting new goals, and periodically reassessing your business plan, you can position your practice for long-term success and sustainability.

IMPLEMENTING ADVANCED BUSINESS STRATEGIES FOR EXPANSION

As your private practice matures and stabilizes, you may find yourself at a crossroads. You've successfully navigated the challenges of establishing your business, and now you're faced with a new question: *How can I take my practice to the next level?* Expansion can be an exciting and rewarding prospect, but it also requires careful consideration and strategic planning.

Understanding Your Motivations for Expansion

When contemplating expansion, it's essential to reflect on your goals and motivations. Are you looking to increase your revenue and profitability? Do you want to serve a larger clientele and impact your community more? Or perhaps you're seeking new challenges and opportunities for professional growth. Understanding your underlying objectives will help guide your decision-making process and ensure that your expansion efforts align with your practice's mission and values.

Scaling Up Operations

One common strategy for expanding a mature practice is scaling up operations. This involves increasing the size and scope of your business to accommodate a more extensive clientele and generate more revenue. Scaling up may entail hiring additional therapists or support staff, expanding your physical office space, or investing in new technology and infrastructure. While scaling up can offer significant benefits, such as increased profitability and the ability to serve more clients, it also comes with challenges. Expanding your team and operations can lead to higher overhead costs, increased complexity in management, and potential quality control issues. It's crucial to weigh these factors carefully and develop a detailed plan to ensure a smooth and sustainable expansion.

Michael, a thriving solo practice practitioner, scaled up his operations by hiring an additional therapist. He carefully considered the financial implications, created a thorough onboarding process, and developed a marketing strategy to attract new clients. Although the expansion process presented challenges, such as increased overhead costs and management responsibilities, Michael successfully grew his practice and was able to serve a more extensive clientele.

Exploring Strategic Partnerships

Another approach to expansion is exploring partnerships with other professionals or organizations. Collaborating with complementary service providers, such as psychiatrists, nutritionists, or wellness coaches, can allow you to offer integrated care and attract a broader range of clients. For instance, you might create a shared care plan for clients, host joint workshops, or refer clients to each other's services to provide holistic support.

Partnering with community organizations, schools, or corporations can involve offering on-site counseling, wellness programs, or employees assistance programs under a contracted agreement. This could include regular visits to provide mental health support, facilitating group sessions or designing tailored programs to meet specific community or organizational needs.

Forging successful partnerships requires finding compatible collaborators who share your values and goals, defining each partner's roles and responsibilities clearly and creating a formal agreement. Regular communication and coordination are crucial for maintaining consistency and ensuring the partnership remains beneficial for all parties involved.

Approach partnerships strategically, ensuring they align with your practice's mission and objectives while enhancing the services you offer and expanding your reach.

Diversifying Your Service Offerings

Diversifying your service offerings is another strategy to consider when wanting to expand your practice. Adding new services or specialties can help you attract new clients, generate additional revenue streams, and foster professional growth. For example, consider offering group therapy, workshops, or retreats in addition to individual sessions.

Developing online courses or resources for self-guided treatment can also provide a scalable and passive income stream. However, diversifying your services requires careful planning and execution. You may need to invest in additional training, certifications, or expertise to deliver new offerings effectively. It's also essential to ensure that any new services align with your brand and core competencies and that you can maintain quality and consistency across all aspects of your practice.

Approaching Expansion Strategically

As you explore these advanced business strategies for expansion, it's crucial to approach the process with a strategic mindset. Expansion should not be undertaken lightly or impulsively but rather with a clear plan and timeline for implementation. This may involve conducting market research to assess demand for new services, developing detailed financial projections to ensure viability, and creating a comprehensive marketing strategy to attract new clients.

Mitigating Risks and Ensuring Sustainable Growth

It's also important to remember that expansion has risks. Growing your practice too quickly or in the wrong direction can strain your resources, dilute your brand, or compromise the quality of your services. It's essential to carefully assess your current situation, resources, and objectives before beginning any expansion efforts. By taking a thoughtful and strategic approach, however, you can mitigate these risks and position your practice for sustainable growth and long-term success.

Making the Decision to Expand

Ultimately, the decision to expand your practice is deeply personal and requires careful consideration of your goals, values, and circumstances. By weighing the potential benefits and challenges of different expansion strategies and developing a well-informed plan for growth, you can take your practice to new heights while staying true to your core mission and values. Remember, expansion is not just about growing your business but about creating new opportunities to serve your clients and make a meaningful impact in your community.

BRANCHING INTO NEW MARKETS

As you consider strategies for expanding your practice, it's important not to overlook the potential for growth beyond the traditional boundaries of one-on-one therapy. Branching into new markets can be an exciting and rewarding way to expand your reach, share your expertise, and make a greater impact in your field.

Speaking Engagements and Workshops

One promising avenue for branching out is through speaking engagements and workshops. As a mental health professional, you possess valuable knowledge and insights that can benefit a wide range of audiences, from community groups and schools to professional organizations and corporations. By offering workshops, seminars, or keynote speeches, you can establish yourself as a thought leader in your field, attract new clients, and generate additional revenue streams.

To identify speaking opportunities, network within your local community and professional circles. Attend conferences and events related to your area of expertise, and connect with organizers to express your interest in presenting. You can also reach out to organizations that align with your mission and values, such as schools, nonprofits, or health care institutions, and offer workshops or training sessions for their staff or clients.

When developing your speaking engagements, consider your target audience and tailor your content accordingly. What are their needs, challenges, and interests? How can your expertise provide value and insight? Be sure to craft engaging, informative presentations that showcase your knowledge and leave a lasting impact on your audience.

Julia, a therapist specializing in mindfulness-based stress reduction (MBSR), began exploring speaking engagements as a way to expand her reach. She started by offering free workshops at local community centers and gradually built her reputation as a speaker. Eventually, she was invited to present at a national conference, which led to new clients and opportunities for collaboration. By strategically branching out to this new market, Julia was able to grow her practice and establish herself as a thought leader in the field of mindfulness-based interventions.

Pursuing Writing and Publishing

Another way to branch out into new markets is through writing and publishing. Sharing your expertise through articles, blog posts, or even a book can help establish your credibility, attract new clients, and generate passive income. Writing also allows you to reach a broader audience and make a lasting impact on your field.

To get started, consider contributing articles or blog posts to publications or websites related to your area of expertise. Many online platforms offer opportunities for mental health professionals to share their insights and reach a wide readership. You can also explore opportunities to write for professional journals, magazines, or newsletters in your field.

If you have a unique perspective or specialized knowledge, consider writing a book or e-book. While the process of writing and publishing a book can be challenging, it can also be a rewarding way to share your message and establish yourself as an authority in your field. To navigate the publishing process, consider working with a literary agent or exploring self-publishing options.

Navigating New Markets

As you explore new markets, it's essential to approach the process strategically and with a clear understanding of your goals and target audience. Before diving in, research your chosen market and assess the demand for your expertise. What are the current trends, challenges, and opportunities in this space? Who are the key players, and how can you differentiate yourself?

It's also important to consider the logistics and resources required to succeed in these new markets. Will you need additional training, certifications, or equipment to deliver your services effectively? How will you market and promote your offerings to reach your target audience? What are the financial implications of branching out, and how will you price your services to ensure profitability?

As you navigate these new markets, be prepared to adapt and evolve your approach based on feedback and results. Seek mentors or colleagues with experience in these areas, and be open to learning from their insights and advice. Remember, branching out into new markets is an ongoing exploration, experimentation, and refinement process.

Expanding Your Impact

Ultimately, branching out into new markets is about more than just growing your business; it's about expanding your impact and making a meaningful difference in the lives of others. By sharing your expertise through speaking engagements, workshops, writing, or publishing, you can touch lives beyond the walls of your therapy office and contribute to the broader conversation around mental health and well-being.

As you consider these growth opportunities, remember to stay true to your core values and mission. Choose ventures that align with your passions and expertise and allow you to serve your audience with authenticity and integrity. By approaching these new markets with a spirit of curiosity, creativity, and service, you can expand your reach and find renewed purpose and fulfillment in your work as a mental health professional.

ONGOING PROFESSIONAL DEVELOPMENT

As a mental health professional, your education and training don't end when you launch your private practice. Continued learning and growth are essential for long-term success in this ever-evolving field. By prioritizing ongoing professional development, you can stay current with the latest research, techniques, and best practices and provide the highest quality care to your clients.

One key aspect of professional development is continuing education. Most states require licensed therapists to complete a certain number of continuing education units (CEUs) each year to maintain their licensure. However, rather than viewing this as a mere requirement, embrace it as an opportunity to expand your knowledge and skills. Seek out courses, workshops, and seminars that align with your interests and areas of specialization and challenge you to grow as a practitioner.

In addition to formal continuing education, consider pursuing advanced certifications or specializations in your field. Specializing in a particular area, such as trauma-informed care, couples therapy, or addiction treatment, can help you stand out in a crowded market and attract clients seeking specific expertise. Pursuing certifications or additional training can also deepen your knowledge and confidence as a practitioner and provide new tools and techniques to enhance your work with clients.

Roberto, a therapist with a general practice, decided to pursue a certification in trauma-informed care. He completed the necessary training and began marketing his new specialization to local organizations and health care providers. As a result, Roberto was able to attract a new clientele and provide more targeted, effective services to his patients. His advanced certification enhanced his clinical skills and set his practice apart in a competitive market.

Another valuable avenue for professional development is attending conferences and joining professional organizations. Attending conferences allows you to learn from leading experts in your field, network with colleagues, and stay up-to-date on the latest research and trends. Joining professional organizations, such as the American Psychological Association or the National Association of Social Workers, can provide access to resources, publications, and continuing education opportunities, as well as a sense of community and support.

Building a strong professional network and engaging in peer consultation or supervision are crucial aspects of ongoing professional development. Cultivate relationships with colleagues in your field, both locally and globally, through attending events, joining online communities, or participating in study groups. These connections can provide invaluable support, guidance, and opportunities for collaboration. Engage in regular peer consultation or supervision to discuss challenging cases, share best practices, and receive feedback on your work. This enhances your clinical skills and helps prevent professional isolation and burnout. Remember, investing in your professional relationships is as important as investing in your formal education and training.

Ultimately, ongoing professional development is about more than just meeting licensure requirements or adding credentials to your resume. It's about a commitment to life-long learning, growth, and excellence in your work. By prior-itizing your education and development, you can provide the best possible care to your clients, stay engaged and inspired in your work, and position yourself for long-term success and fulfillment in your career.

PRIORITIZING PERSONAL GROWTH AND WELL-BEING

While focusing on professional development is crucial for the success of your practice, it's equally important to priori-tize your own personal growth and well-being. As a mental health professional, you spend your days caring for others and holding space for their struggles and challenges. However, to be truly effective in your work, as we discussed in chapter 11, you must also take care of yourself and invest in your own personal development.

One key aspect of personal development is enhancing your leadership skills. As a private practice owner, you are not only a clinician but also a leader and entrepreneur. Developing skills such as effective communication, decision-making, problem-solving, and team management can help you navi-gate the challenges of running a business and inspire confi-dence and trust in your clients and colleagues.

Another important aspect of personal development is improving work-life balance. The demands of running a private practice can be all-consuming, and it's easy to fall into the trap of working around the clock and neglecting your own needs and relationships. However, maintaining a healthy work-life balance is essential for preventing burnout, maintaining your mental and physical health, and modeling self-care for your clients.

To improve work-life balance, set clear boundaries around your work hours and stick to them as much as possible. Make time for hobbies, exercise, relaxation, and social connections outside work, and prioritize your self-care practices, such as meditation, journaling, or therapy.

Speaking of self-care, maintaining your mental and physical health is perhaps the most important aspect of personal development as a therapist. As the saying goes, you cannot pour from an empty cup, and taking care of yourself is essential for being fully present and effective in your work with clients.

This means prioritizing your own therapy or counseling when needed, practicing stress management techniques, getting enough sleep and exercise, and nourishing your body with healthy food and hydration. It also means setting boundaries around your workload and saying no when necessary to prevent overextension and burnout.

In addition to these practical strategies, personal development also involves cultivating a growth mindset and a commitment to lifelong learning and self-reflection. This means being open to feedback, seeking out new experiences and perspectives, and continually challenging yourself to grow and evolve as a professional and as a person in general.

Ultimately, personal development and well-being are not just nice-to-haves but essential components of a thriving and sustainable private practice. By prioritizing your own growth, self-care, and balance, you can show up more fully and authentically in your work with clients and create a successful, deeply fulfilling practice that aligns with your values and purpose.

REINFORCING CAPABILITY AND POTENTIAL FOR SUCCESS

As we near the end of this journey, it's important to take a moment to reflect on how far you've come and the incredible potential you hold for continued success. Throughout this book, you've acquired a wealth of knowledge and skills that have prepared you to navigate the challenges and opportunities of running a thriving private practice.

You've learned how to cultivate an entrepreneurial mindset, embracing innovation and calculated-risk taking as essential tools for growth. You've gained financial literacy and an understanding of managing your practice's finances and creating sustainable revenue streams. You've mastered the art of effective messaging and communicating your unique value proposition to attract your ideal clients. You've developed strong practice management skills to ensure that your business runs smoothly and efficiently. And perhaps most importantly, you've built resilience, learning to navigate setbacks and challenges with grace and determination.

These skills and knowledge are theoretical concepts and powerful tools you can apply daily in your practice. They form the foundation of your success and will continue to serve you as you grow and evolve as a practitioner and business owner.

As you move forward, remember to embrace challenges as opportunities for growth and innovation. Every obstacle you face is a chance to learn, adapt, and come out stronger on the other side. Trust in your abilities and have faith in the solid foundation you've built. Your potential for success is limitless, and your dedication to your craft and clients will continue to set you apart in this field.

INSPIRING CONFIDENCE AND CONTINUED EVOLUTION

As we conclude this chapter and this book, I want to leave you with a final message of inspiration and empowerment. You have chosen a path that is both challenging and deeply rewarding, one that allows you to make a profound difference in the lives of others. Your decision to start a private practice took courage, dedication, and a belief in yourself and your ability to succeed. As you continue on this journey, hold on to that belief and let it guide you through the ups and downs of entrepreneurship.

Remember that your evolution as a practitioner and business owner is an ongoing process. There will always be new skills to learn, new challenges to face, and new opportunities to explore. Embrace this continuous growth and approach it with a spirit of curiosity, openness, and self-compassion.

You now possess the tools, knowledge, and mindset to build a thriving practice that supports your financial goals and aligns with your deepest values and purpose. You have the power to shape your career and life in a way that brings you joy, fulfillment, and a sense of making a difference in the world.

As you step into this next phase of your professional journey, do so with confidence, knowing that you are capable of achieving extraordinary things. Surround yourself with supportive colleagues and mentors, and never hesitate to reach out for guidance or support when needed. Remember that you are part of a community of passionate, dedicated mental health professionals who are all working toward a common goal of helping others heal and thrive.

Above all, trust in yourself and your vision for your practice. Your unique talents, experiences, and perspective are needed in this world, and your work has the power to transform lives. As you continue to grow and evolve, stay true to your core values and your commitment to making a positive impact. The journey ahead may not always be easy, but it will be filled with opportunities for growth, connection, and profound fulfillment.

So go forward with courage, confidence, and an open heart. Embrace the challenges and triumphs, the setbacks and breakthroughs. And know that with each step you take, you are not only building a successful practice but also creating a legacy of healing and hope that will ripple out into the world in countless ways.

REFLECT AND TAKE ACTION

As we conclude this transformative journey through the world of private practice, it's important to take a moment to reflect on the insights, strategies, and tools you've gained along the way. Throughout this book, we've explored the myriad aspects of building and growing a successful therapy business, from cultivating an entrepreneurial mindset and developing effective messaging to mastering practice management and navigating the challenges of the work.

Key Takeaways
- Sustaining success in private practice requires maintaining an entrepreneurial spirit, even as your business becomes more established. This involves regularly setting new goals, staying updated with industry trends, and periodically reassessing your business plan.
- Expanding your practice can take many forms, from scaling up operations and exploring strategic partnerships to diversifying your service offerings. Each

approach offers unique benefits and challenges; the most suitable path depends on your specific goals and circumstances.

- Branching into new markets, such as speaking engagements, workshops, and writing or publishing, can be a powerful way to expand your reach, establish your expertise, and create additional revenue streams. Success in these ventures requires strategic planning, market research, and a willingness to adapt and refine your approach.

- Ongoing professional development is essential for long-term success and fulfillment in private practice. This includes pursuing continuing education, advanced certifications, and specializations, attending conferences, joining professional organizations, and staying current with the latest research and best practices in your field.

- Personal development and well-being are just as crucial as professional growth. Prioritizing self-care, work-life balance, and your own mental and physical health is essential for preventing burnout, maintaining your effectiveness as a therapist, and modeling healthy practices for your clients.

Action Steps

1. Set aside time to create a detailed road map for the next phase of your practice's growth. Identify specific goals for the next one, three, and five years, and break these down into actionable steps with clear timelines.

2. Conduct a SWOT analysis of your practice, assessing its current Strengths, Weaknesses, Opportunities, and Threats. Use this analysis to inform your decision-

making around expansion strategies and potential new markets to explore.

3. Develop a comprehensive professional development plan. Research and select at least three continuing education courses, workshops, or certifications to pursue in the coming year. Set aside a dedicated budget and schedule these activities.

4. Create a personal well-being plan. Identify the self-care practices, hobbies, and activities that nourish and recharge you, and commit to integrating these into your routine. Set firm boundaries around work hours and time off to ensure a healthy work-life balance.

5. Reflect on your purpose and values as a therapist and business owner. Craft a personal mission statement that encapsulates the impact you want to make and the legacy you hope to leave. Let this mission serve as a guiding light and source of inspiration as you continue to grow and evolve in your practice.

As you begin this next chapter of your journey, remember that building a thriving, fulfilling private practice is an ongoing process of learning, growth, and self-discovery. The tools and strategies you've gained from this book will serve as a solid foundation, but your ultimate success will come from your ability to adapt, innovate, and stay true to your unique vision and values.

Embrace the challenges and opportunities that lie ahead with curiosity, courage, and a commitment to positively impacting the lives of your clients and your community. Surround yourself with supportive colleagues and mentors, and never hesitate to reach out for guidance or encouragement when needed.

As you continue to grow and thrive in your practice, remember that you are part of a vibrant, global community of therapists united in their commitment to helping others lead happier, healthier, and more fulfilling lives. Together, we have the power to create a brighter, more compassionate future for all.

So go forth with confidence, knowing that you have the skills, the wisdom, and the heart to build a practice and a life that are truly extraordinary. Embrace the journey ahead, and know that you are making a difference in the world with each step you take.

ABOUT THE AUTHOR

Nancy Cowden is a licensed marriage and family therapist (LMFT) and business coach with twenty-five years of experience in mental health. For the past twelve years, she has successfully run her own prosperous private practice. Passionate about increasing access to care, Nancy founded Ravel Mental Health, an online provider directory and booking platform that makes it quicker and easier to find a therapist and schedule appointments.

Her mission is empowering clinicians to launch fulfilling, profitable practices that make a meaningful impact while achieving work-life balance—a challenge she has navigated as a business owner and mother. Nancy shares expert strategies developed from her entrepreneurial journey to guide therapists in building sustainable private practices.

In her free time, you can find her spending quality time with loved ones, working out, relaxing at the beach, and indulging in a good book. Drawing from her unique clinical expertise and business skills, Nancy provides invaluable mentorship to help mental health professionals establish thriving private practices.

www.ingramcontent.com/pod-product-compliance
Lightning Source LLC
Chambersburg PA
CBHW030458210326
41597CB00013B/710